CONFESSIONS OF A FEMALE RABBI

CONFESSIONS OF A FEMALE RABBI

RELEVANT RELIGION IN AN ON-DEMAND WORLD

RABBI REBECCA KEREN JABLONSKI

Viva
EDITIONS

Published in the United States by Viva Editions, an imprint of Start Midnight, LLC, 221 River Street, Ninth Floor, Hoboken, New Jersey 07030.

Printed in the United States
Cover design: Jennifer Do
Cover photo: Alex Koralkovas
Author photo: Rina Gluckman
Text design: Frank Wiedemann

First Edition.
10 9 8 7 6 5 4 3 2 1

Trade paper ISBN: 978-1-63228-097-8
E-book ISBN: 978-1-63228-119-7

To where I come from:
Grandma Rev and Grandpa Jack Eisenstadt
Merry and David Eisenstadt

CONTENTS

NOTE FROM THE AUTHOR

The following is a historical memoir. This book reflects the accuracy with which I remember events and conversations. In some sections, places, names, and identities of families or clients have been changed to protect the anonymity of individuals. In those cases, I've combined stories and events from multiple families. While very few of my families ever ask me to sign non-disclosure agreements, I retell all stories understanding the delicacy of family privacy and reflect their information with respect.

The confessions are my honest admission that give insight to my personal introspection and assessment. The confessions reflect my inner conflicts and my truth, including that sometimes, even as a rabbi, I do things out of the religious norm.

The verses from the scripture are taken from the original Hebrew text and translated by me or otherwise listed.

The essays, speeches, and *divrei Torah* are the words of the author listed and composed for the lifecycle event the client or their family member was observing, unless otherwise noted.

CONFESSION I:
I think about Jewish survival now more than ever

"I will grant peace in the land, and you shall lie down untroubled by anyone; I will give the land respite from vicious beasts, and no sword shall cross your land."
LEVITICUS 26:6

It hit me about fifteen days into the 2023 Israel-Hamas war exactly *why* my phone was ringing off the hook, pinging with requests, and exploding with emotional messages.

American Jews and their allies felt completely gutted by a surprise barbaric attack that left more than 1,200 Israelis murdered by Hamas, a terrorist organization whose mission is Jewish genocide.[1] Israel's version of 9/11 took place on October 7, 2023, a holy holiday that also fell on *Shabbat*, the Sabbath. The holiday weekend, *Shemini Atzeret* and *Simchat Torah*, is dedicated to rejoicing over the Five Books of Moses that give Jews their foundational stories and our 613 commandments that dictate Jewish life. Hamas' massacre was unleashed on a significant, traumatic anniversary, falling fifty years and a day after the start of the Yom Kippur War

---

1   Wilson, Rachel, et al. 2023. "These Charts Show the Scale of Loss in the Israel-Hamas War." CNN, November 7, 2023. https://www.cnn.com/2023/11/07/middleeast/palestinian-israeli-deaths-gaza-dg/index.html.

in 1973.[2] The violation of our holiest of times is only one example of the heinousness of the assault. There would be countless stories of Jewish farming families in *kibbutzim*, communal villages, that were tortured, shot, burned, beheaded, and kidnapped. Thousands of young concert goers attending the Nova Music Festival, coined "a journey of unity and love," in the nearby area were ambushed.[3] Hundreds of victims were brutally murdered and others were raped or kidnapped.[4] Soldiers and police were attacked on their bases. Bodies were dragged and seized into Gaza, then beaten and defiled by mobs in the streets. Victims included babies, Holocaust survivors, peace activists, mothers, children, fathers, teenagers, and pregnant women. There were Bedouins, Arabs, foreign workers from the Far East, and other non-Jews among the dead, injured, and captive. Citizens of thirty-three countries were among an estimated 239 hostages abducted by terrorists into the dark, dank maze of terror tunnels in Gaza.

I couldn't sleep the night leading into October 7th. I was spending the holiday weekend officiating at the bar mitzvah service for my second cousin, Luke Dreifuss. Besides the family connection, I had decided to teach and mentor Jackson and Luke, the two young boys of my first cousin, Josh, for one main reason: their birth mother, Randi, tragically died from cancer when

2   Elving, Ron. 2023. "Israel's Battle with Hamas Recalls Yom Kippur War and Its Fateful Effects." NPR, October 20, 2023. https://www.npr.org/2023/10/20/1207015189/israel-hamas-yom-kippur-war.

3   Sherwood, Harriet. 2023. "How the Hamas Attack on the Supernova Festival in Israel Unfolded." *The Guardian*, October 9, 2023. https://www.theguardian.com/world/2023/oct/09/how-the-hamas-attack-on-the-supernova-festival-in-israel-unfolded

4   Gettleman, Jeffrey, Anat Schwartz, and Adam Sella. 2023. "'Screams Without Words': How Hamas Weaponized Sexual Violence on Oct. 7." The *New York Times*, December 28, 2023. https://www.nytimes.com/2023/12/28/world/middleeast/oct-7-attacks-hamas-israel-sexual-violence.html

the boys were very young. She was one of the most special and loving older cousins I had. I remember having a conversation with Randi at my sister's wedding, and in a rare moment of pessimism, Randi expressed sadness that she'd never see her children under the *chuppah*, marriage canopy, or even have a bar mitzvah. My cousin, Josh, was a saint during her entire illness.

Josh was lucky to fall in love again and remarry an incredibly dynamic and caring woman, Toula. Toula was of Greek descent, and not Jewish. What a hard role for Toula to step into: while she had her own sons and a fresh divorce, Toula was now a coparent to Josh's two young boys who craved a maternal presence. Toula often says that she mothers Jackson and Luke with Randi in mind every day. Still, there was a small part of me that could hear the worries of my ancestors: *could a non-Jewish woman raise Jewish children?* She has proven to be more than capable. I just wanted to add my support and help with the boys' Jewish education.

As I lived in New York and they lived in a Washington, DC suburb, weekly Zoom sessions bonded me to Jackson and Luke during COVID-19. Besides reinforcing the Hebrew and prayers they had learned at their synagogue's Hebrew school and camps, I taught the boys their Torah portions and worked on their sermons with them. I told them stories about their great-grandparents, grandparents, and parents. I showed them pictures of me with their parents, and of them as babies with their mother, Randi. I reminded them of the importance of Jewish values from not just a rabbi, but a *cool* cousin.

Jackson had an intimate in-home ceremony that was live streamed during the pandemic. I colead with his synagogue rabbi, who was present only through a giant TV screen. While there was notable physical and emotional distance from their synagogue, I made up the difference by being their rabbi on-site.

For their younger boy, Luke, the family chose a venue independent of the synagogue and hosted a weekend retreat at their "happy place"—the boys' overnight Jewish summer camp. I managed all of Luke's teaching and planning and officiated at services. Luke was a great student as he was motivated, smart, and musical. He recognized many prayers having already learned them at home, Hebrew school, and camps. Our work was focused but easy. At the end of every Zoom session, Luke would tell me that he loved me.

The crisp October bar mitzvah weekend was hosted in the mountains of Waynesboro, Pennsylvania on the grounds of the Capital Retreat Center. I felt removed from my regular urban life—including strong Wi-Fi. Our family members had traveled from Washington, DC; Maryland; Virginia; North Carolina; Georgia; Massachusetts; and California. My then-fiancé, Ben, was meeting my extended family for the first time, but was late due to flight delays in Las Vegas.

I drove five and a half hours from New York City with my dog, Scout, and four cans of my favorite energy drink, CELSIUS. The car was packed with various Jewish artifacts needed to lead the ceremonies. The Friday night ceremony was basically a joyous cousin reunion of sixty relatives singing Shabbat prayers followed by a traditional kosher dinner. The evening was capped by a peaceful bonfire around which we all told stories about the bar mitzvah boy, sang John Denver folk songs, and roasted kosher marshmallows to make s'mores. I went to bed exhausted from the driving and a little tense about my rabbinical duties for the next day. The eerie mix of silence, rain, and crickets chirping all night was totally different from my usual city soundscape of sirens and honking cars outside my window.

At 7:32 a.m., realizing I wouldn't fall back asleep, I finally looked at my phone. I had a message from my mom:

> Sat, Oct 7 at 6:22 AM
>
> Stay calm but israel declared a war, just so you know.

Ben and I began reading horrible news on our phones, most of it confusing and unclear, about Hamas rocket attacks; a Gaza border infiltration via air, land, and sea; hostages; and *kibbutz* communities being overrun by terrorists. I immediately messaged my best childhood friend's father, former Israeli Ambassador to the European Union, and NATO (The North Atlantic Treaty Organization, also called the North Atlantic Alliance), Ronny Leshno Yaar. He lives with his wife, Debbie, in a Jerusalem suburb and I wanted to check on him, especially to see how far-reaching distress was in Israel. He said a rocket had fallen on his street and there was total chaos. I don't think any of us realized just how serious everything else was yet. Ben and I quickly reached out to the rest of our family and close friends that live in Israel. Many of them were confused and sheltered in place.

In disbelief, I went to get a cup of coffee in the main lodge. My cousins were just waking up and didn't want to discuss, but my aunts and uncles were all on high alert and seemed to understand how grave the situation would become. Focused on the bar mitzvah, I had to rehearse Luke one last time. As part of the holiday, I also had to roll the very heavy Torah scroll from the very end all the way to the start for Luke's reading of The Story of Creation—*Bereshit,* in the beginning. Everything seemed so dramatic and biblical. We were reading about the start of everything and unthinkable destruction was unfolding in the Middle East. By the time I was geared up to lead the service, I knew that the death count was rising rapidly.

With my cousin, Josh, we decided the service would proceed as planned, but I made an announcement very early on that our hearts were with Israel as we pray for peace. Since Luke studied at a public school in Virginia, there were several families in attendance that had never been to a bar mitzvah ceremony. I made a point of mentioning that every traditional Jewish prayer service includes our fervent hope, "May the One who makes peace on high bring peace among His people and all Israel. And let us say: *Amen.*" Instead of the congregation reading the *Prayer for the State of Israel* together, Josh wanted his mom's best friend, Jackie Haines, to come forward alone. Her usual smile was replaced with furrowed brows, displaying deep worry.

Luke and his family were able to maintain joy and focus to achieve an amazing and happy bar mitzvah service. He did a great job, and we were all so proud of him. I was only half present. I was freezing cold, sweating, and shivering with emotions. I wore my Bandolier crossbody phone strap, and immediately checked my phone after the service. This is something a rabbi typically wouldn't do on the holy Sabbath or a holiday, especially because the camp administration had required observing Sabbath rules.

The death toll had risen and there were news reports about many hostages. After a quick lunch, Ben and I went back to our room and watched videos of kidnapped women being paraded around Gaza, one alive, with blood stains between her legs, and one face down in a truck, possibly dead. I would later learn that the names of those girls are Naama Levy, a nineteen-year-old peace activist and the great-granddaughter of Holocaust survivors who had just started her military service; and Shani Louk, a twenty-three-year-old German-born tattoo artist, who was an avowed pacifist and did not serve in the Israeli military under conscientious objector status. Two months later, Louk was confirmed dead by recovered fragments of her skull at the Nova festival site; on

May 17, 2024, Israeli forces finally rescued her lifeless body that had been held in Gaza for more than 200 days.[5]

The rest of October 7th is a blur. My whole family was glued to their phones and CNN was turned on at the camp office. Huddled with my parents and the elders of the family, Ben and I tried to make sense of *how* or *why* this could happen. Ben and my father understood the "why now?" better than anyone and explained to others who asked. In my role as rabbi, some of the young or non-Jewish guests asked me what was going on, as if I had the answers. Jackson asked "What was going to happen to the hostages? What did Hamas want from them? How long was this war going to last?" My heart broke knowing many of the hostages would be tortured, sexually abused, or murdered.[6] I also felt sick knowing many innocent Palestinians would die as Israel would pummel Gaza to try to extract the hostages and neutralize those responsible.

Ben and I ended the weekend early, decidedly not dancing at the party. In a state of shock and sadness, we made our way back to New York City. We listened to news the entire car ride home. I spoke to my best friend, Noa, and she told me dozens had been kidnapped to Gaza—that it wasn't just a few. Dozens? *Dozens?!* Oran, her husband, would tell us that his father went out armed to protect and guard their *moshav* village, a few kilometers from Gaza.

I had no time to process my own fear or grief. I had lessons scheduled for all of Sunday, October 8. Being back in NYC, I grabbed my iPad, my large flag for the State of Israel, energy

---

5   Mesa, Jesus. 2024 "Where Shani Louk's Body Was Found." *Newsweek*, May 17 2024. https:// 5 www.newsweek.com/shani-louk-hostage-body-hamas-israel-oct-7-1902044

6   Kingsley, Patrick, and Ronen Bergman. 2024. "Israeli Hostage Says She Was Sexually Assaulted and Tortured in Gaza." The *New York Times*, March 26, 2024. https://www.nytimes.com/2024/03/26/world/middleeast/hamas-hostage-sexual-assault.html.

drinks, and Lara bars. Still, I wound up canceling the second half of the day's lessons—too upset and depleted to do my job.

Everyone needed me to explain what was happening. A few parents told me their children were afraid to *be Jewish* and I had to explain to a pair of elementary school siblings why they could still feel pride in Israel and being Jewish even though people wanted to kill us. I had to watch my language. I had to reach adults, teens, and kids, yet monitor maturity levels and appropriateness. There were no trending articles yet on "How to Talk to Your Kids or Students About Genocidal Terrorists Coming for You and Your People." I used my big Israeli flag as a teaching tool: the star represents the courage of King David who fought a big giant even as a small boy, and eventually made Jerusalem our capital more than 3,000 years ago. I recounted that the flag is blue and white to represent the colors in the garments of the ancient priests, or *Cohanim*, and stripes represent our religious prayer shawl, or *tallit*. I reminded the students and families in my sessions that I always have worn my "Mazel Ring" made by artist Rachie Shnay: it is a big Jewish star on my most prominent finger, and on the back portion is engraved with *Am Yisrael Chai*—two meanings, "The Jewish People Live" and "The Nation of Israel lives."

As the week went on, alerts and messages from groups on every possible social platform relentlessly flew in, and my phone became a command center. I was hearing directly from students and families that I served in the present and past: "How are you?" "What is happening?" "Where are you and are you safe?" "Do we know anyone who is hurt?" Requests of all kinds flooded in from Israeli family, friends, and colleagues. They needed money, nonmilitary equipment, and supplies. My network of successful Jews or sympathetic allies were asking: "Where should we send money?" "What was the immediate need?" "Could you help organize multiple charter planes full of medical aid for the wounded or emergency centers?" "Who knows of a plane leaving tonight from New York that can take duffel bags full of supplies for troops?" "What would be a good Palestinian aid charity to help the emerging humanitarian crisis that guarantees resources don't fall into the hands of Hamas?" "Could you link a donor with a commander asking for new uniforms, backpacks, and water bottles for an entire elite unit tasked with recovering hostages?" "Can you recommend a children's hospital in Israel for those interested in donating only to children's causes?"

The focus of questions also spread to ensuing hate and tension unfolding outside of Israel. Many Jews felt vulnerable all over the world. I had to explain and update constantly, validate fears, and simultaneously calm mass hysteria. "Was there a credible threat to Jews in New York City?" "Was this about terrorism, religion, or land?" "What is a day of rage?" "What river and what sea?" "Why is the world so quick to start defending the terrorists or justify the violence?" "Why does Israel need to have a defense for defending itself?" "Why has antisemitism erupted on college campuses?" "Why won't the high schools and primary schools handle the subject properly?" "If Israel doesn't feel safe and we don't even feel safe in the US, where do we go?" "Who are these Jewish fringe groups to immediately denounce Israel or call for a ceasefire without any rescue or return of the hundreds of hostages?" "How can we honor the innocent people and children dying in Gaza while still being proud Jews?" "Why has Gen Z abandoned the Jews?" "Why does no one have real information?" "What do we do?"

Why was I, an independent rabbi in Manhattan, suddenly consumed with this war? Through my phone, I felt like I was fighting a double front war for our people's survival. The first most immediate need was to raise enough money for support, gear, and medical supplies in Israel. The second need was to keep Jews informed and prideful about wanting to be Jewish, whether religious or cultural. I did not concern myself with explaining to our critics and enemies why Israel has the right to exist or defend herself. I resisted the rabbit hole of fighting the thousands of online antisemites and human rights hypocrites. Don't get me wrong—I saw them; they boiled my blood and broke my heart. Yet, I had always designated my social media for PG-rated religious messages of solidarity and Jewish joy, and given the wide-range of my follower's ages, I was very cautious when sharing graphic details that would increase fears. Moreover, Ben and I agreed that people were only speaking into their own echo chambers and there was no real dialogue or information sharing between opposing sides. Existing social media warriors like Noa Tishby, Eve Barlow, Hen Mazig, and Lizzy Savetsky took on the impossible battle and made inroads. Instead of speaking into deaf ears and posting to the blind eyeballs on social media platforms, I chose to use my efforts for concrete action.

One of the greatest parts of our religion is the obligation to give charity. The first days of the war, I personally donated to United Jewish Appeal (UJA)-Federation of New York Israel Emergency Fund, American Friends of Israel's Navy Seals (AFINS), Magen David Adom First Responders (MADA), and Emergency Aid for the Southern Communities—so I directed people there at first. Many of my clients gave as part of the historic millions raised for UJA at Park Avenue Synagogue or Central Synagogue on the first Shabbat after October 7th. For the first time in their lives, many of my clients decidedly went to a synagogue on a non-holiday Friday. In times of crisis, people tend to turn to one another for support. Whether this strengthened Jewish solidarity will affect formal synagogue membership and/or sustained participation is difficult to ascertain at present.

Still, extraordinary Jews wanted to be more hands on, and they didn't relate to what these huge charities were doing, *tachles—*

bottom line. I was heartened that so many within my network wanted to give in enormous ways or spring into action. I was inspired by legends of about "Banana Man," Sam Zemmary, or future Prime Minister Golda Meyerson/Meir, both US Jews who helped to support or fundraise for Jewish refugees and the State of Israel through her troubled inception—prior to the Holocaust, during the crisis of displaced survivors post-war, at the time of the historic United Nation's 1947 Partition Plan vote and throughout the Independence War of 1948. WhatsApp was mission control for coordinating funding, materials, and supplies for the hundreds of thousands of Israelis who were displaced by the war. Groups of successful Israelis, many secular, felt like they had the know-how, military connections, and logistics backgrounds in order to coordinate big grassroots efforts that would meet immediate needs they were hearing about from their friends and family on the ground in Israel. Those Israelis would reach out to me to help direct American charity dollars or private donations to their efforts. There was vigilance against getting scammed or worse, that terrorists were listening. Everything was urgent, important, and disorganized. This was not some organized cabal of prominent Jewish leaders, as the *Washington Post* suggested in its May 16, 2024 antisemitic article about Jewish billionaires using money and power to influence NYC Mayor Eric Adams.[7] Instead, this was a scrappy effort from caring Jews and allies of all income levels, trying to alleviate Israeli suffering after the largest attack on Jews since the Holocaust.

The most successful grassroots effort I witnessed was titled Team *Ima*, Team of Mothers. My two clients (and friends), Meredith Sotoloff and Tracy Weiner, banded together in every way possible

---

7   Natanson, Hannah and Emmanuel Felton. 2024. "Business titans privately urged NYC mayor to use police on Columbia Protesters, chats show." The *Washington Post*, May 16 2024. https://www.washingtonpost.com/nation/2024/05/16/business-leaders-chat-group-eric-adams-columbia-protesters/.

when they mobilized their wallets, homes, cars, and Amazon Wish Lists, sending duffel bag after duffel bag full of supplies or necessities requested by their contacts in Israel. First, Meredith turned her kitchen into a challah baking factory to raise money. I even cohosted a challah bake event to raise funds for expensive state of the art emergency medical equipment. If that wasn't enough, Meredith and her aunt created a logistics network of mothers in New York and partnered with Meredith's friend in Israel, Michal "Mickey" Yoran. They have gotten protective gear and supplies to various units of IDF (Israel Defense Forces), toys to children, breast pumps to new mothers, and so many other items to those in need. Tracy has joined Meredith's effort, turning part of her Upper East Side home into a literal warehouse. Tracy and Meredith joined the Park Avenue Synagogue mission to Israel and flew over to volunteer less than two months after the war started. In this traumatic moment, they came together as best friends. I should mention, Tracy was born and raised as a Christian, but with her Jewish husband, she raised her children to be practicing Jews. Tracy committed to a Jewish conversion even prior to October 7th. Team Ima's generosity knew no bounds. I take no credit for their giving and spirit. Sometimes when I needed help sending bags or items, I leaned on Meredith and Michal. Every now and then, they also relied on me, the concierge rabbi, for extra direction or support.

Why were these small groups doing such a great job of meeting the immediate needs of our people in Israel? Why were we hearing from Israelis on the ground that they lacked critical gear even though institutions were saying they were sending supplies? How could the Israeli government and military be so unprepared? How could the main diaspora charities raise millions yet still not meet the needs weeks into the war? Why did people feel good about going around the large institutions?

Also, pertaining to inflamed campus antisemitism, Jewish

students were under verbal and physical attack and the organizations in place couldn't do enough to protect their Jewish
members or stop the actions of perpetrators. By December of
2023, a congressional hearing with three prominent university
presidents (University of Pennsylvania, Massachusetts Institute of Technology, and Harvard University) attempted to hold
the schools and leaders accountable for their inaction.[8] Certain
prominent figures felt urgency and wanted to bypass the
drawn-out, consensus-seeking process that larger communal
institutional groups follow. Instead of going through estab-
lished organizations that traditionally have advocated for Jews
on campuses, one by one impactful individual charges were
leveled. High net-worth business people like Jon Huntsman,
Bill Ackman, and Marc Rowan were finally speaking up and
addressing the widespread campus antisemitism and failures
in leadership. Alumni were taking meetings with their school
associations and withdrawing financial support in a visible
way. They didn't make their statements through the Anti-
Defamation League (ADL) at a huge conference, or through
Israel on Campus. They simply released statements via social
media. Similarly, like efforts were not limited to only the
wealthy. Workers at large companies in a variety of positions
were outraged by vague statements not strongly condemning
Hamas; this was particularly evidenced by documented HR
complaints at Condé Nast. In the immediate aftermath of
October 7th, before any military operation started in Gaza,
US Jews publicly demanded that their workplaces take a stance
to support Israel and denounce terror—the same way the

---

8   Treisman, Rachel. 2023. "Lawmakers Grill the Presidents of Harvard, MIT and
     Penn over Antisemitism on Campus." NPR, December 5, 2023. https://www.
     npr.org/2023/12/05/1217459477/harvard-penn-mit-antisemitism-congress-
     hearing.

companies did during the outbreak of the Russia-Ukraine war or Black Lives Matter (BLM) movement.[9]

The answer to all of these *"whys?"* hit me.

We were let down by institutions at large. The United Nations; federal, state, and local governments; businesses; popular culture icons; and secular schools all had subpar or weak turnout for the Jews. What's worse? We also have a crisis within.

Religious institutions have been failing to engage modern Jews for the last several decades and the war highlighted people's lack of direct involvement and commitment. Statistically, Jews outside of the Orthodox world have been less and less engaged with their synagogues and community centers. Up to half of the US Jewish adult population does not attend synagogue; more than fifty percent of that cohort say they find other ways to express their Jewishness outside of the Synagogue.[10] We'll get into the numbers, supporting studies, and facts later in Confession II. The need for community never left Jewish people, but it was substituted by people's colleges, children's schools, and workplaces—all in which they invested time and money. For a while these places were sufficient sources of supportive community. American Jews found life-long friends in universities and the workplace. Some even found their spouses in those spaces. Many of those friends and partners were Jewish too, so it really felt like a Jewish community at college or work—especially in popular fields among Jewish people. Jews also spend exorbitant sums of money on their children's schools,

---

9   Lincoln, Ross A. 2023. "Conde Nast CEO Condemns Hamas Attacks After Initial HR Statement Draws Staff Complaints." Yahoo! News, October 11, 2023. https://malaysia.news.yahoo.com/conde-nast-ceo-condemns-hamas-212657611.html.

10   Pew Research Center. 2021. "Jewish Americans in 2020." Pew Research Center, (May 2021): 23. https://www.pewresearch.org/religion/2021/05/11/jewish-americans-in-2020/.

teams, and camps. Those microcommunities, along with gyms, have replaced the need for many people to have a relationship with Jewish institutions like synagogue or UJA.

According to the Pew Research Center, while sixty-seven percent of Jewish adults identify with some branch of US Judaism, only thirty-five percent of US Jewish households are members or have a person who is a member of a particular synagogue.[11] The aging synagogue and institutional model of Judaism has been waning for some time, forcing many congregations to merge, or close for good.[12] Historically, modern Jews have preferred to get their "Jewish fix" for decades by celebrating a few holidays a year at their parent's home, watching sitcoms like *Seinfeld* and *Curb Your Enthusiasm*, or taking a Birthright Israel trip once in their lives.

However, the Israel-Hamas war revealed that Jews need more community and support. If someone had a synagogue membership, they went there in the weeks right after the attacks. Many Jews reported a feeling of unity among other Jews after October 7th. Unfortunately, history proves these acts of solidarity are often short lived. Plus, pluralistic work and school communities fell short to support Jews. Like other minority groups, we have unique needs that cannot be fully met by secular social groups. Jews are a part of an ethno-religious group that deals with wave after wave of antisemitism or hate. Thus, these places failed to meet Jews' needs as Jews.

After October 7th, poisonous latent or down-right blatant

---

11   Ibid, 44.

12   Knopf, Rabbi Michael. n.d. "What's Driving Jews Away From Synagogues? Not Dues, but 'Membership.'" *Haaretz Daily Newspaper Ltd.* https://www.haaretz.com/jewish/2016-05-26/ty-article/.premium/membership-is-stopping-jews-from-paying-synagogue-dues/0000017f-e9ab-d62c-a1ff-fdfb9d8d0000?lts=1707236787849.

antisemitism was unleashed in and around those communities. By the spring of 2024, the college encampment movement, a thinly veiled anti-Jewish and anti-Zionist campaign started at Columbia University. Pro-Palestinian encampments popped up at more than fifty US college campuses and even more abroad. While some were peaceful demonstrations of solidarity with the Palestinian people against Hamas and perceived Israeli military aggression, an over-whelming amount of the encampments included vandalism, threatening hate speech, demands for boycott and divestment from Israel and her supporters, and out-right violence against Jewish students and faculty. Hundreds of protesters were arrested for violation of university rules, damage to property, and even taking over campus buildings; this included the daughter of Squad member, Ilhan Omar, a Minnesota congressional representative. Many graduation and commencement ceremonies were canceled due to the disruption and safety warnings. After conducting a survey of Jewish American students, the president of Hillel International, Adam Lehman, said: "Jewish students, and all students, deserve to pursue their education and celebrate their graduations free from disruption, antisemitism, and hate." That survey found that sixty-one percent of Jewish students who witnessed a pro-Palestinian protest at their school found that they have included language that is antisemitic and threatening.[13] New York City was riddled with protests and counter solidarity efforts. Widespread synagogue bomb threats, vandalism including spray painted swatstikas and broken windows of Jewish businesses echoed events of *Kristalnacht*, Germany's Night of Broken Glass in 1938. Jews expressed their

---

13 Lapin, Andrew. 2024. "Many Jewish Students Say Pro-Palestinian Encampments Make Them Feel Less Safe Hillel Survey Finds." Jewish Telegraphic Agency. May 13, 2024. https://www.jta.org/2024/05/13/united-states/many-jewish-students-say-pro-palestinian-encampments-make-them-feel-less-safe-hillel-survey-finds

outrage and confessed fears that even worse was still to come. Local law enforcement couldn't protect Jews and universities were once again breeding grounds for antisemitic ideology like they were in Europe in the 1930s. Anti-Zionsim (the belief that Israel has no right to exist and Jews have no right to self-determination in their ancestral homeland) had largely become the foremost form of anti-semitism, even among well-meaning liberal educated elites. None of the Jewish or secular institutions in place were enough to restore order, reassure community safety, or even emotionally support the millions of Jews in the United States.

Ironically, many participants of the encampments were actually Jewish and members of fringe groups like Jewish Voices for Peace (JVP) and Students for Justice in Palestine (SJP). Liberal Jewish journalist, Peter Beinhart, with whom I generally disagree, suggested in his Substack that many progressive students went from being non-Zionists (people who's political ideas had nothing to do with Israel) to being against Israel once their conscious-nesses turned to the suffering in Gaza. They misplaced all blame on Israel's Jews. They ignored that this is a two-sided conflict. They did not make mention of decades of corruption, provoca-tion, and violence encouraged by the Iranian backed terror groups who use innocents as their shields. Beinart discussed a civil war within colleges amongst Jews. Orthodox or observant Jews, first generation Jews, those enrolled in professional schools, or involved in Greek life trend more pro-Israel than the Jewish liberal arts students, LGBTQ+ Jewish students, or Jewish students who have assimilated and forgotten Jewish history. [14]

When little to no action was seen to combat or stand against

---

14 Beinart, Peter. 2024. "Six Observations about the Campus Protests." Substack. May 6, 2024. https://peterbeinart.substack.com/p/six-observations-about-the-campus?utm_source=share&utm_medium=android&r=a61zs&triedRedirect=true&initial_medium=video

Jew hatred from college leaderships and boards, many felt betrayed or lost. My clients and I felt disappointed more than ever that their communities would not do enough to support them during this awful war. Worse, many of those beloved institutions outed themselves to be unfriendly to Jews and breeding grounds for antisemitism and hate. This war's devastation hit much harder among unaffiliated Jews or Jews with loose ties to a home base. If they did not feel a strong connection to a Jewish institution with Jewish values and interests at its core operating principles, American Jews felt like they had nowhere to turn.

The November 14 March for Israel rally in Washington, DC was attended by nearly 300,000 Jews; in part, it was so packed because it allowed Jewish people a physical space to come together on a national scale and express solidarity, anguish, and purpose. This feeling of empowerment was deeply needed and could only be achieved by feeling the warmth and unity of Jewish community. May this serve as a reminder: Jewish organizations can band together in exceptional times and become nimble enough to organize individuals into collective action, as evidenced by the huge turnout from participants affiliated with large groups and those who heard about the rally through social media and came on their own.

By the way, have we heard anything from Vice President Kamala Harris's Jewish husband? Doug Emhoff, the first Second Gentleman, had no problem tokenizing his Jewishness when it served him on campaign trails or for party propaganda, but he was notably absent from the November 14 solidarity march right outside his door on the Washington Mall. He has posted absolutely nothing religiously related since Hanukah, December 2023 other than an Easter egg hunt—nothing about Passover, the foundational Holiday marking the inception of Jewish national and religious identity. He may have championed the first ever US

National Strategy to Counter Antisemitism in May of 2023, but when push came to shove it was all lip service or self-serving. As of May 2024, he's been publicly silent about the five American citizens who remain hostages in Gaza (let alone the rest of the 120 hostages). Unless brought by private groups, he's been invisible during the calls for intifada in major cities and campus encampments "tentifadas." His own daughter does not consider herself Jewish or even half-Jewish. The opposite. Ella Emhoff reportedly fundraised for United Nations Relief and Works Agency (UNRWA), a group that sixteen nations have stopped funding due to their documented terror ties.[15] Ben thinks my criticism of Doug Emhoff is too extreme, but my outrage in his lack of public advocacy is indicative of how the many institutions, even those with Jew-ish members, fell short.

AND SO, as an independent provider, my services were needed more than ever. I was always an alternative to people who were turned off by standard or big-box religious offerings. I was often used as a supplement to make up for where an institution was lacking. As a private rabbi, I was on-call at all hours of the day, to teach and facilitate people coming together under our faith's umbrella. And that's even before the war. After October 7th, I was in-demand to explain the conflict, the implications, and break it all down in terms anyone and everyone could understand. I helped CEOs draft statements to demonstrate support and set a tone at their workplaces. I advised about large donations. I invited people to the emerging events, rallies, and tribute nights to raise money

15 Levine, Jon. 2024. "Kamala Harris' stepdaughter Ella Emhoff publicly raising money for relief group allegedly tied to Oct. 7 terrorist attack on Israel" *New York Post*, March 16, 2024. https://nypost.com/2024/03/16/us-news/kamala-harris-stepdaughter-ella-emhoff-publicly-raising-money-for-unrwa-despite-alleged-terror-ties/

for supplies and equipment. I became supplementary to synagogue institutions' prayer groups and lecture series. I was nonstop explaining thousands of years of Middle East history. I was on the phone all the time. I would validate someone's concern for safety and try to quell hysteria. I'd hear someone's desire to help, meet them where they were at, and pull them through. There were other rabbis, philanthropists, and dedicated people like me, mobilizing independently. The big organizations were obviously fundraising and trying to make a difference too. But their structures were both bureaucratic and opaque, which combined to reveal slow or ineffectual action. I teamed up and leaned on many others for help in this unprecedented war effort. The reason we were so needed, especially the independent leaders, was because of this huge shift in American religion.

The center of religious identity is moving. The coming chapters in this book suggest that this change is all part of a larger pattern not to be ignored—that is if we want to survive.

So, who am I and *why* should you care? I'm Rabbi Rebecca Keren Eisenstadt—oh now Jablonski—but you can call me Becky. I'm a young, Jewish woman from Maryland with a strong Jewish identity and values. But I've been living in Manhattan for twenty years and I've learned how to adapt to the world as it has changed. As Julia Gergely's award-winning profile in the Jewish Telegraphic Agency stated, I'm the "*Uber* of rabbis."[16] I'm not just a religious provider who meets people in their homes, I meet people where they are at; I see where they want to go and devise a plan to get them there. And I make the process interesting, meaningful, and fun—as it *should* be. However, a major difference between Uber and my services is that

---

16   Gergely, Julia. 2022. "This Private, On-Demand 'Hot Rabbi' May Soon Be the Star of Her Own Reality TV Show." Jewish Telegraphic Agency, May 25, 2022. https://www.jta.org/2022/05/25/ny/this-private-on-demand-hot-rabbi-may-soon-be-the-star-of-her-own-reality-tv-show.

your Uber driver is a one-off and I'm not. Uber is a transactional business and I often make a lasting bond with my client. Nonetheless, ride sharing apps make finding reliable transportation seamless and I make religion accessible and more available than your average American clergy. Also, my model is bespoke, boutique, and personal with each person or cohort I serve. That recipe is what's in-demand to take people on various spiritual journeys and remain active and prideful during these dark times.

With nearly two decades working for mostly New York-area clients, I have created a niche with some of the most prominent families in the world. I started out as being one the most sought-after Hebrew and bar mitzvah preparation tutors in the tristate area. When I attained rabbinic ordination, my services expanded to weddings and more, like baby namings, funerals, and conversions. According to the Jewish religion, almost every lifecycle moment can be performed by simply a knowledgeable person—it doesn't have to be a rabbi. Still, most of my clients feel more comfortable having a rabbi oversee religious moments and I've been extremely busy ever since I earned my official title. Sometimes, I call it my sash and crown. I've been blessed to watch some children grow since they were literal babies and continued to advise them as they navigated campus life and antisemitism outside of New York. I've become more than just a clergy member to families; I'm integrated into a family which allows us all to mutually care for one another. I am present for a family's happiest occasions and saddest moments. I am with them on vacation, at parties, and in their homes while they are wearing pajamas on the weekend. The institutional demands and expectations of most formal synagogues do not allow for pulpit clergy to have such informal roles and availability.

Most of the time when I reveal that I'm a rabbi, people are shocked. I'm a one of a kind religious leader—party planners call me the "Hot Rabbi." My Instagram handle, @myhotrabbi, has thousands of followers from every walk of life. I'm the only rabbi around town with super long hair, makeup, and can be seen wearing either workout clothes while carting around my little shih-poo (that's a shih tzu-poodle mix) dog, Scout, or decked out in a ball gown for a fabulous celebration. For a while, I was also single and people loved setting me up, or hearing about the trials and tribulations of New York City single life through the eyes of someone Jewishly-observant. Thank heavens, as of March 2024, I am married to the most wonderful man, who has been my friend for seventeen years. After meeting at a Shabbat dinner and getting closer through his foundation, Building Together (Palestinians and Israelis building relationships together through farming and economic development), Ben Jablonski finally asked me out, and in less than a year, we were engaged in Jerusalem—the same place my parents got engaged.

People constantly come up to me asking for advice for their families, children's learning, or how to integrate more religious values into their homes. Frankly, for a long time, I wasn't ready to tell my story of how I became a rabbi to serve a need in the Jewish community. I used to think I was doing something wrong by helping people have services apart from the traditional model or away from their synagogues. But my views have evolved. Now, I see how people crave meaningful experiences that are different and personal. I'm ready to share and perhaps inspire other families to seek out similarly meaningful experiences. I also want to encourage Jewish leaders to become providers like me. I never instruct people to discontinue their synagogue memberships. I can add value, supplement, or make up where others' needs or preferences are not met. Religion is not one-size-fits-all—to carry the clothing metaphors—no one has a closet full of only one brand of clothes. When I grew up, I was used to going to several synagogues and had many rabbis as teachers. I want to remind American Jews that they can and *should* have multiple religious providers in multiple institutions. Now the numbers of people leaving the traditional ways of observance and membership are so large, I feel like I'm playing a part in keeping families still engaged in their Jewishness. I'm a totally new model of clergy or rabbi in the US. In her best selling book, coauthored by former NFL player Emmanuel Acho, titled *Uncomfortable Conversations with a Jew*, secular Israeli activist Noa Tishby explains her favorite parts about Judaism. "It's a decentralized religion. Meaning you don't really need a single designated place, such as a synagogue, to practice it. Our temples had a nasty habit of being destroyed, and Jews tended to be kicked out of most places they lived. So Judaism went through a sort of rebrand that made the community the center of the sacred, as well as the individual—meaning (most of) our rituals could travel with us and be just as sanctified." Tishby reminds us that ever since the destruction of the First and Second Temples in Jerusalem, Judaism has evolved. Judaism can be practiced individually and includes a big tent of multiple religious denominations, observance levels, and providers.[17] I am a leader in the decentralized and post-denominational era.

Moreover, to know me, you don't have to leave your house and pay membership dues. Most of the time you see a religious leader in formal attire or costumed on a platform or stage. Most parishioners, especially Catholics and Jews, are used to passively watching their preacher high up on a pulpit and dressed in ritual garb. Often the congregation is silent while the clergy leads, chants, and performs words of worship for all. By the way, the clergy is almost all male, even though there has been a growing number of female rabbis since the late 1970s.[18] This keeps many feeling distant from

---

17   Acho, Emmanuel and Noa Tishby. 2024. *Uncomfortable Conversations with a Jew*. Simon Element, April 2024.

18   Cohen, Debra Nussbaum. 2022. "Transforming the Rabbinate Over 50 Years." HADASSAH, March 2022. https://www.hadassahmagazine.org/2022/02/28/transforming-rabbinate-50-years/.

the leaders, religion, and G-d itself. I have heard complaints of synagogues and churches being tired and stale. Patrons who turn to me have previously felt like they were one of the sheep, among the masses, obligated like everyone else to attend and be bored—and they pass that dreaded experience to their children. With me, I dress and act like the people I serve. I purposely balance the formal and informal, sitting on their floor and standing on the religious stage with my clients. I lead with songs they recognize and know from their communities and upbringings.

I am a goal-oriented rabbi and my goal is to *get Jewish*.

I hate labels. I say I'm nondenominational. Sometimes I say I'm "Hipsterdox," which means I'm hip and cool about a lot of things and strict about others: you've got to stay contin*jew*ed to figure out what I mean. I live every part of my life this way. I've always cared that the Jewish people continue to thrive alongside their neighbors. I care about the continuation of our traditions as an ethnic group and religious people. I know the only way to do this is to appeal to people through their hearts and emotions, but back everything up with facts. I try to find what they are missing and deliver it in a fun and meaningful way. I build a lasting connection with each of my clients and help them realize how they are fulfilling something great in the chain of our people and in themselves through our work together. I believe most congregational rabbis hold similar aspirations and heartfelt intentions; they are limited by organizational structures and role expectations of an esteemed rabbi.

Enjoy the book: *Am Yisrael Chai*

CONFESSION II:
We have greatly sinned in what
we have done and what we have failed to do.

"Make for yourself a teacher, and acquire for yourself a friend;
judge all people with the scale weighted in their favor."
—MISHNA AVOT 1:6

I remember exactly where I was sitting in Mrs. Yelnick's tenth grade Jewish History class when I found out that Jews were 0.2 percent of the world's population. That's only 0.002 of the roughly eight billion people in the world. I felt the air tighten around my face as my bubble burst and I realized there were less than fifteen million Jews alive in the world in 2001. A bunch of my classmates laughed at me, as I was the only one out of twenty-two students in the room who did not know that statistic. I always knew how important it was to keep Jewish people Jewish, affiliated, and proud, but my insular life of religious schooling and synagogue kept me cloistered and ignorant. Ever since then, life outside the bubble has been totally different. I have understood the urgency with which Jewish leaders and teachers instill the importance of living Jewishly.

But I've got news for the Jews—and all the other religions— the census and majority of research in the US show we've had a major decline in retention, affiliation, and participation in religious communities. It's at least a little nice to know we aren't alone; this exodus is not isolated to one religious faction. In the new book, *The Great Dechurching*, by Jim Davis and Michael

Graham, the authors estimate that 40 million Americans have de-churched or left various forms of the Christian Church in just the last twenty-five years.[19] What's really interesting about the de-churched, they point out, is that while people may leave church, they still have a basis and memory of church and practice. Many of those people still maintain belief, identity, and some level of practice at home. However, the next generation of children will be considered unchurched, meaning that they have no religious affiliation and exposure. When one generation leaves, the next generation grows up with even less affiliation and less statistical likelihood of coming back. The Survey Center on American Life reported in a study on generational religious trends in 2022 that thirty-four percent of Gen Z are not affiliated with any religion. This is compared to eighteen percent of baby boomers and nine percent of the silent generation.[20] According to the same study, "Less than one quarter (twenty-four percent) of Americans overall report that they attend religious services once a week or more often, while over half (fifty-three percent) state that they seldom or never attend services."

Likewise, a 2014 Gallup poll showed that eighty-two percent of American adults believe in G-d, seventy-six percent identify with some Christian religious group, and yet fifty-three percent attend a religious service at least monthly. But, just fifty-seven percent of Americans claimed they are a member of any specific religious body, and on an average week, a mere third of American adults

19 Davis, Jim, and Michael Graham. 2023. *The Great Dechurching: Who's Leaving, Why Are They Going, and What Will It Take to Bring Them Back?* Zondervan, 3.

20 Cox, Daniel A. 2022. "Generation Z and the Future of Faith in America." The Survey Center on American Life, March. https://www.americansurveycenter. org/research/generation-z-future-of-faith/.

will attend church.[21] The membership number was already down to forty-seven percent in Gallup's 2020 study which reported that the growth of the religiously unaffiliated "nones," those who claim no religion, has directly impacted membership numbers across faiths; "nones" grew from eight percent in 1998–2000 to twenty-one percent in 2018–2020. "The two major trends driving the drop in church membership—more adults with no religious preference and falling rates of church membership among people who do have a religion—are apparent in each of the generations over time."[22] Reading all this makes it clear, something in the institutional model of religion—of which I am a product, the model I've known and loved—is failing.

I don't mean to be a *kvetch*, a complainer, but the numbers are worse for the Jews than they are for the other groups. More than half of American Jews say they never go to synagogue. There's real data. That same study in 2022 by American National Family Life claims just four percent of Jews attend services once a week or more while fifty-seven percent report attending religious services "seldom or never." In analyzing this stark information, politics Professor Samuel J. Abrams of Sarah Lawrence College wrote: ". . . Jews are not particularly religiously engaged by most traditional metrics which opens the question of what it means to be Jewish in America today."[23] The Pew Center for Research's 2020 study on Jewish Identity and Belief reports that fifty-two percent

---

21 Newport, Frank. 2014. "Three-Quarters of Americans Identify as Christian." Gallup, December. https://news.gallup.com/poll/180347/three-quarters-americans-identify-christian.aspx

22 Jones, Jeffery M. 2021. "Church Membership Falls Below Majority For First Time." Gallup, March 29, 2021. https://news.gallup.com/poll/341963/church-membership-falls-below-majority-first-time.aspx

23 Abrams, Samuel J. 2022. "Jewish Religious Exceptionalism." The Survey Center on American Life, April. https://www.americansurveycenter.org/jewish-religious-exceptionalism/.

of its respondents said that being Jewish had to do with ancestry.[24] Likewise, fifty-five percent reported that being Jewish had to do with culture, either alone or in combination with some of their other answers. Only thirty-six percent of respondents say that the religion has to do with Jewish identity "suggesting that most US Jews do *not* see being Jewish as primarily about religion." The rest of the Pew numbers would make my mother rip her garments in mourning. "Religion is not central to the lives of most US Jews. Even Jews by religion are much less likely than Christian adults to consider religion to be very important in their lives (twenty eight percent vs. fifty-seven percent)," Pew stated. It was hard to pick out the most important numbers to share here, because I find the study so fascinating. What's more alarming: only one in five Jews find meaning in their religion. When the same group was asked, fifty-three percent of Jews said religion is "not too" or "not at all" important to them personally. In the study there are pages and pages of data, percentage rates broken down by denomination and age. The bulk of my statistics comes from different sections of the Pew 2020 report "Jewish Americans in 2020" unless noted otherwise. If you are really interested in the depressing numbers, I invite you to read the full study.[25]

We are at a really interesting time in American culture—pluralistic egalitarian views have swept the country for decades during a time of massive industrial and technological innovation. It makes complete sense that what worked for the baby boom generation sixty years ago is outdated for the times. We've seen local stores and providers merge or close due to big box stores and online consumerism. Companies merge or fail, and likewise so have places of worship. Religion News Service's Bob Smietana

---

24 Pew Research Center, "Jewish Americans in 2020," 62.

25 Ibid.

published a new study in 2022 titled "Reorganized Religion: The Reshaping of the American Church and Why It Matters." In a panel hosted by the American Enterprise Institute discussing his claims with *Washington Post* Religion reporter Michelle Boorstein, the University of Connecticut's Ruth Braunstein, and Trinity Forum's Peter Wehner, Smietana said:

> Old people go to church, young people don't. And the old people are going to die out and if the young people are not going to replace them, we are going to decline . . . The other thing that has happened in America that's happened that people don't pay enough attention to is the local congregation is closed. It's shrunk. The consolidation means we have half of Americans in really big churches. So all the people are in these really big churches that are run by a few leaders who are human beings, and are going to fail and those congregations are really weak. We see these big mega churches, you think 10,000 people, people think: "oh that's awesome." They go to church less, they volunteer less, they give less, they give very little tithe. The back door is as big as the front door. So we have weakened the local, closely tied congregation ties. We have built really big institutions that are really weak and we have built them on really weak people and they are not up to the pressures they are dealing with from the outside.[26]

Smietana pointed out the self-defeating paradox religion faces: local congregations cannot survive because only older people are attending church and they are dying out, and yet, when churches

---

26 American Enterprise Institute. 2022. "Reorganized Religion with Bob Smietana | LIVE STREAM." December 2, 2022. https://www.youtube.com/watch?v=ziPG7GYfwMI&t=584s.

merge and become larger, they are actually weaker and do a poorer job. They seem to be well attended because the seats are full, but in actuality, the attendees have a revolving door of loyalty. Megachurches do not have as deep a meaning in people's lives. I'll draw a comparison between religious houses and Broadway. I used to work in Broadway producing and understand the numbers game—we looked at audience house reports every morning. All too often a great show that couldn't find its audience would be considered a flop and close. Many times, shows that were more commercial and tourist appealing sold well but lacked depth.

This is why when you go to any institution, the leaders are constantly obsessing over membership and continuity. If you ask most religious leaders, they have workshops and conferences to brainstorm for effective ways to insure meaningful participation in spiritual programing. They try to engage members with numerous ways to keep annual subscriptions. Film screenings, museum trips, religious classes, cooking workshops, pilgrimages to Israel, and charity projects within the community are all ways to get people out of the passive pews and living religious life. *The Amen Effect*, by Rabbi Sharon Brous, attributes "The disengagement crisis . . . not unique to Judaism" as a driving force behind the 2004 creation of Ikar, her progressive and vibrant synagogue community in Los Angeles.[27] As one of the most influential Rabbis in the country, Brous has scaled her work with a successful book, TED Talk, and employing a variety of other strategies to inspire within her sacred community and beyond. Yet with secular culture so alluring, we haven't hit the nail on the head. We've missed the mark—which is the same way in Hebrew to say we've sinned. A *heyt* or an *aveirah*, a sin, is not considered some mortal bad deed,

---

27 Brous Sharon, 2024. *The Amen Effect: Ancient Wisdom to Mend Our Broken Hearts*. Avery, an imprint of Penguin Random House, New York.

but trying to do something and missing the goal. Rabbi Brous experienced at the turn of the millennium what decades prior Rabbi Abraham Heshel blasted: "Religion declined, not because it was refuted, but because it became irrelevant, dull, oppressive, and insipid." For more than half a century, we've been off target as religious providers, as the numbers reflect.

Before I go on—I just want to make sure we all have the same lingo. There are different denominations of Judaism just as there are in other religions. I don't tend to agree with my very religious brother-in-law, but he would say, "There's Orthodox and then there is everything else." Orthodox Jews adhere most strictly to the Jewish religion and its restrictions. They are comprised of Hasidic *Jews,* like you see in the streets of Williamsburg with the hats and the long beards; *Haredi Jews,* all over Queens, Brooklyn, and Israel outwardly wearing yarmulke head coverings; Modern Orthodox Jews like Jared Kushner; and just traditional Orthodox. which might include Sephardic traditional Jews. They are the most recognizable Jews wearing yarmulkes, keeping kosher, observing the Sabbath, and living in more insular neighborhoods. As of 2020, Orthodox Jews made up nine percent of American Jewry,[28] but I believe the number is on the rise due to birth rate and relative retention rates.

But not everyone wanted to stay adherent or strict after the European Renaissance and enlightenment of the 1700s, and so the Reform movement was born in Germany in the early 1800s. Reform Judaism modernized the religion. It revised the need for strict adherence to Jewish law and stressed the importance of social justice. Reform Judaism accounts for thirty-seven percent of American Jews. Some circles joke that, given the principles

---

28   Pew Research Center, "Jewish Americans in 2020," 14.

taught by Jesus, he was actually the first Reform rabbi. Founded in the mid-nineteenth century, Conservative Judaism was a reaction in some ways to Reform Judaism being too loose. Conservative Jews make up eleven percent of American Jews, however their group is in the decline due to mergers and school closures. Still, Conservative and Reform Judaism have a lot in common, that is, they now allow for same sex marriage, female clergy, mixed gender seating, instruments, and technology used during the services, and a handful of other rules that are seen as blasphemous to the Orthodox. Intermarriage is still a big debate—and only the Reform movement finds it permissible. There are other denominations that make up about four percent of American Jewry. If you added up all those percentages, we still have a huge portion of Jews unaccounted for; those Jews are unaffiliated with any one movement and they are still really important to my work. Most of this chapter relates to the non-Orthodox denominations. Orthodox Judaism, has more immunity to the changes described.

With intermarriage rising from forty-five percent to seventy-two percent since the late 1980s among non-Orthodox Jews, some feel the religion's dilution or disappearance.[29] Conservative thought leaders point to the many statistics that demonstrate if children are raised with only one religion they are more likely to continue practicing that religion. It makes sense—beyond the confusion of Hanukkah and Christmas presents, or Easter Sunday after a Passover *seder*, if you believe in Judaism, how can you also believe that Jesus is the son of G-d or the Messiah? Yet interfaith marriage has left the station, and there are no hopes in turning that train around. Love is love, and in this day and age, you can't convince someone not to marry the partner they desire. According

---

29   Ibid, 39.

to the Pew 2020 survey, "Nearly two-thirds of US Jews (sixty-four percent) say rabbis should perform marriage ceremonies for interfaith couples (that is, between someone who is Jewish and someone who is not), and an additional twenty-five percent say 'it depends.'"[30] While not every rabbi would agree with me, the overwhelming trend with modern Jews is to welcome interfaith couples.

This is not a new problem, mind you. Even Tevye, the father in *Fiddler on the Roof,* dealt with the intermarriage issue of his daughter Chava, who fell in love with the Russian Orthodox soldier Fyedka. That story, *Ṭeyye der Milkhiḳer,* or, *"Tevye the Milkman,"* was originally written in 1895 by Sholem Aleichem. Aleichem wrote stories in Yiddish about the dilemmas Jews faced at the turn of the nineteenth century in Russia and Poland. Only part of *Ṭeyye der Milkhiḳer* was turned into *Fiddler on the Roof,* a Broadway musical first produced in 1964, written by Joseph Stein. The stories were given killer songs like "To Life" and "If I were a Rich Man," which I would sing with Grandpa Jack practically every time I visited with him. Whether we are in biblical times, 1895, 1964, or 2024, it's all the same problem: as the world and traditions change, some stick and some don't. With *options* comes *choice.* Jewish people partner with those outside of their own faith because the option is available and attractive. Instead of fighting against intermarriage, Central Synagogue's Rabbi Angela Warnick Buchdahl suggested in a somewhat controversial Yom Kippur sermon in 2023, that we must be more welcoming to the non-Jewish people that are helping to partner and build Jewish families, whether through conversion or intermarriage. "The persistent mandate to marry someone Jewish is not the only path towards Jewish continuity, nor is it sufficient. It may even be backfiring. You see, the American Jewish community

---

30   Ibid, 47.

has been saying this for over seventy years, but it hasn't stopped our children from falling in love with people who aren't Jewish."[31] Buchdahl goes through history from the prophet of Ezra's stance on intermarriage in Babylon in 450 BCE to the reform Jewish leader Rabbi Alexander M. Schindler's revolutionary 1978 plan of outreach and welcoming of intermarriage families. Rabbi Buchdahl recounted first hand that Rabbi Schindler's plan helped her family have a stronger sense of belonging and ultimately led her to become a rabbi. She mentioned many of Central's clergy are products of intermarriage as well—and this is one of the biggest synagogues in the world! Nevertheless, her Korean-American mother never fully felt welcome to convert. The message: we should do a better job as a religion bringing closer the people who are instrumental partners to Jews. Rabbi Buchdahl's point was to highlight those who are dedicated to the synagogue system whether or not they are actually Jewish.

Bringing in new Jews is hard enough, so most institutions focus on existing members and the time during which members are most engaged—when they have young children. It is every parent's wish to pass down values and traditions to their children. Synagogues and Jewish Community Centers have great programming for early childhood, so much so that I have two friends who are devout Christians who send their children to Jewish Community Centers for pre-schooling (in different metropolitan areas). Through supplementary and mostly after-school religious school with focus on ethics and prayers, it seems like families are being led to the ultimate moment: the iconic coming of age ceremony of bar mitzvah—a young adult accepting the commandments with a

---

31 Central Synagogue. 2023. "Your People Are My People | Rabbi Angela Buchdahl | Kol Nidre 5784." September 26, 2023. https://www.youtube.com/watch?v=rhFSYRXrgf0.

ceremony and party. As Jews love metaphors, a common symbolic strategy is now employed by synagogues: at almost every bar and bat mitzvah service, clergy line up the parents and grandparents of a child and physically pass the Torah scroll down the line of living relatives. This tender moment—with a twinge of guilt in there too—expresses that all who came before the child participate in this great chain and the expectation is continued participation from this child. But symbolically passing a twenty-pound hand-written book hasn't been enough to keep away assimilation, apathy, and flat-out rejection of Judaism. The statistics are in-line with all other faiths. Jewish observance, with the exception of the ultra-religious community, is in decline hand over fist. And in thirty years, the numbers will be even more stark since the next generation will grow up with little to no exposure to places of worship.

Simply put, *shul* (synagogue): US Jews are just not that into you! Why have people been leaving? Let's break it down. While the authors of *The Great Dechurching* are mostly interested in cataloging the crisis of membership within the Evangelical Church, the dilemmas are the same in Reform and Conservative Judaism. The main reasons why people are leaving their churches fall under two categories: casual indifference to religiousness or some traumatic event that repelled them from the church. Casual indifference could be related to the changing of times: technology, urbanization, over scheduling, and feeling that a religious lifestyle lacks daily relevance. In a section of their study labeled "Why Jews go, or don't go, to religious services," Pew reports that US Jews who do not attend shul clocked in as sixty-seven percent as "just not religious," fifty-seven percent as "just not interested," and fifty-five percent as "expressing their Jewishness in other ways."[32] This

---

32 Pew Research Center, "Jewish Americans in 2020," 23-24.

was exacerbated when the COVID-19 pandemic shut the doors of institutions and peoples' weekend worship time became filled with other things. Even now that homes of worship are open for business or even accessible online, people have replaced the significance of those places in their lives. People also find community in places with members of different faiths; they are interested in multicultural pluralism and inclusive experiences. The traumatic or repelling events could be anything from a perceived dramatic issue with the clergy or the church organization, ethical and even sexual misconduct by church members, a strong difference in political affiliations, and even perceived bigotry and racism. Polls track the decline of affiliation to the Catholic Church's tough stances on the LGBTQ+ lifestyles and their sex abuse scandals. This is more than just a squabble in a church subcommittee, or a disagreement with the board president. There are real documented abuses or coverups of religious officials in every denomination. That immoral behavior is downright hypocritical and has ruined thousands of people's chances of belonging to any religious institution.

A good friend of mine also mentioned the financial element of belonging to a faith-based organization in America that seemed off-putting and traumatic. We had a conversation during *Sukkot,* a weeklong annual festival when Jews mark how temporary our blessings are through building and living in a temporary hut. We enjoy fresh fruits from the fall harvest. We observed the holiday by shaking the branches of special trees with an expensive sixty-dollar *etrog,* or citron fruit that looks like a lemon. We laughed at the frivolity of it all. With economic times bleaker than ever for the middle class, feeling a need to pay for spirituality feels wrong. All the research tells you those who are successfully churched are members of typical American nuclear family households (households in which both parents and children exist under one roof). Various Christian churches survive generally on tithing and donations; synagogues and community centers operate based on memberships and donations. That construct is tenable for the classic American family dynamic. Both types of institutions end up giving a lot of attention and respect to members who not only pay dues, but contribute additional time and money. There are some Spanish/Sephardic/Persian synagogues that have auction bidding for honors during services, motivating people that if they want a high honor and recognition, they must donate money. As I grew up in traditionally European-style synagogues, I only experienced this for the first time in my twenties and on Long Island. Even I was totally shocked—I can't imagine how someone would feel if they were struggling financially or just less committed to Jewish life. Likewise, anecdotally, when I asked one of my young students how High Holiday 2023 services were for him, he answered: "The rabbi just talked about ChatGPT for his sermon and invited a parade of rich people up on the stage. I think we could have gone up, but we didn't." It makes sense that institutions would be grateful to their donors, but at the same time, this signals to the average member that standard membership is not enough. Moreover, single people find the membership pricing very steep and are often embarrassed to ask for financial assistance. Plus, statistically they may not even be so sure about the institution's importance in their lives. Single people establish places of community outside of their religious home bases. It's all a tragic numbers game. Inevitably, they will meet a partner outside of their religious faith. Neither one of them will feel at home in the walls of a religious institution. It will be even harder to convince a young couple of the need to join an expensive institution if it wasn't such a big part of their lives before, let alone if the place isn't engaging or only caters to the rich members, or members with kids. Understandably, Pew's "Jewish practices and customs" study reported that seventeen percent of US Jews stated cost as the reason for their lack of attendance.[33]

It's clear that American Jews no longer rely on shul solely for their community. In 2020, The Harvard Divinity School hosted a webinar with Dean Lori Stevens and alumni, Casper ter Kuile and Angie Thurston, who now work as millennial religious leaders. Kuile discusses how increasingly, millennials rarely attend a religious institution, and supplement with various social or recreational activities that the individual finds meaningful and spiritual. "So you're seeing a kind of mixing and kind of remixing of these different places to form an individual unique set of experiences and communities. However, the downside of that is the more it becomes personalized, the less it's shared. And so that's one of the drivers for us that's been pushing towards this theme of social isolation." Kuile points to how CrossFit gyms, with their rituals and rigorous training schedule, are a church replacement and "becomes the social hub of people's lives."[34] Listen, I worked for the cultish spinning studio, SoulCycle, for four years. Many people used to joke that spin class was like their "spinagogue." Interestingly, when I worked for SoulCycle, customers would complain there was no monthly membership—but that was part of the beauty of SoulCycle. You had to keep investing and coming back to get something out of your time and money. That constant re-upping of resources and attendance built loyal members. Contrast that with the economic model of a gym (and probably a synagogue): getting people to pay annual membership dues. Like everyone, people commit to good habits on

---

33 Ibid, 83.

34 Harvard Divinity School. 2020. "Video: Religion for a New Generation." https://hds.harvard.edu/news/2020/04/02/video-religion-new-generation.

the new year (*Rosh Hashanah* for the Jews) and then slack on attendance or real participation as the year goes on. That's what helps the gym and synagogue make money and keep so many members.

And then there are online and technological advances that have replaced our needs for religion. While many people find healthy online communities, some also use the platforms to share fringe beliefs or explore outside their religion of origin. Through the Internet, a person can find someone just like them with similar beliefs and struggles with one religious context and swap out one belief system for another. And that includes atheism, a belief that the stories about G-d and religiousness are not valid or are untrue, thus the resulting doctrine is not worth following. Endless modern options that fulfill the need for community have replaced the church and synagogue.

So, because of interest, time, money, and feelings, people just aren't showing up. But that doesn't mean they still don't feel Jewish or even practice religion at home or with friends. I would classify this era for Jews as the great "de-shuling." People are leaving or seeking supplemental Jewish experiences outside the synagogue. Life no longer centers around the community center and place of worship. After an independent survey of one hundred families I served between the years 2020–2023, I discovered my clients are right in line with everyone else in America. Only fifty-seven percent of the families I serve currently hold membership with a synagogue, and fourteen percent never had a membership to begin with. So, if you do the math, that means that twenty-nine percent of my families have dropped their synagogue in recent years. Only five percent have dropped membership completely after the pandemic. Sixty-two percent of the families I serve have voiced dissatisfaction at some point with their synagogue with which they have a membership. My clients overwhelmingly sought my services because of my flexibility of approach, location, and timing, at seventy-one percent. Simply put, people want more flexibility with what they want, and when they want it. They want access to something religious in the home or office. I also tracked that thirty-two percent of the families I serve have a make-up other than the typical two-parent heteronormative marriage. Some consist of same-sex couples, interfaith couples, and many include a divorce or stepfamily that complicate the picture.

Thirty-nine percent of the students that I work with have some documented form of a learning challenge or disability. As of 2024, The International Dyslexia Association stated that between fifteen and twenty percent of the population have a language-based learning disability, with dyslexia being the most common.[35] Between ADD (attention-deficit disorder), ADHD (attention-deficit/hyperactivity disorder), dyslexia, and other forms of language-based learning disabilities, a one-size-fits-all Hebrew school cannot be right for everyone. Rabbi Moshe Waldoks of Brookline, Massachusetts wrote in JewishBoston: "When the Temple was destroyed by the Romans in 70 CE, the synagogue became more vitally central to the establishment of Jewish communities all over the world. Synagogues were also called *batei tefila*, or houses of prayer, and *batei midrash*, or houses of study. In Eastern and Central Europe, this led to the synagogue being called a shul, the Yiddish word for school."[36]

---

35 The International Dyslexia Association, Inc. n.d. "Frequently Asked Questions." The International Dyslexia Association, Inc. Accessed January 2024. https://dyslexiaida.org/frequently-asked-questions.

36 Waldoks, Rabbi Moshe. 2012. "What's the Difference Between a Temple, a Synagogue and a Shul?" *JewishBoston*, July 10, 2012. https://www.jewishboston.com/read/whats-the-difference-between-a-temple-synagogue-and-a-shul/.

People would learn within their synagogues—both about the religion and the holy language of Hebrew. Yet, if a huge percentage of students have documented behavioral challenges or learning disabilities, with mostly untrained and unaccredited educators, how can Hebrew school really be effective at teaching? Thus, I have heard time and time again from clients that they are pulling their child out of Hebrew school because their child learns next to nothing. Then, many people no longer see the need to use their shul at all—if not for school and educating their children. More to the point, if the school doesn't work, then the shul or synagogue eventually loses members and closes. According to a recent study by the Jewish Education Project, a nonprofit that supports Jewish educators, total enrollment in Hebrew school which often goes by the title of Jewish supplementary schools, dropped by forty-five percent from 2006 to 2020. Nearly half of the Hebrew schools in America have closed.[37]

Growing up, I didn't even enroll in Hebrew school because I was part of a Jewish day school—a dual language curriculum private school. Learning about Judaism and Hebrew was included in my daily studies. For me, synagogue was a place for worship, community events, holidays, and a weekly meal after services. Nonetheless, the long carpeted halls of my shul, Congregation Beth El of Bethesda, Maryland, and even my grandparents' shul, Ohr Kodesh Congregation in Silver Spring, Maryland, felt familiar, casual, and easy. I belonged there; the joyous memories of my childhood years are linked to the predictable schedule of religious practice and affiliation. But something has largely shifted in my millennial generation and in Gen Z. The vast majority don't actively belong to an institution and miss out on the associated

---

37 Contreras, Russell. 2023. "Hebrew School Enrollment in U.S. Drops Sharply." Axios, May 4, 2023. https://www.axios.com/2023/05/04/hebrew-schools-enrollment-in-us-drops-sharply.

benefits of attendance like improved emotional wellbeing and lower rates of anxiety.[38]

As far as religious leaders are concerned, the *de-shuled,* or actively *de-shuling,* are totally off the map. They have their hands full in engaging their community as is. Executive directors and rabbis have to deal with their current boards, engagement, programs, and the lifecycle moments of their congregants. Occasionally, when an institutional rabbi learns I'm working with one of their prominent members, they look embarrassed, as if they were caught off guard that their congregant was in need of supplemental instruction or inspiration. If you talk to any rabbi, they are typically drowning in their schedule. I know I am. They are so busy with appointments and overextended in their own lives. Anecdotally, Rabbi David Ingber of Romemu in New York City made his whole Rosh Hashannah 2023 speech about this topic and quoted the Coldplay song "Fix You." The entire congregation sang along with projected lyrics about trying hard and falling short. However, the rabbis and their staff have a model that keeps them barely afloat only *with* the people who are still involved, paying, and seemingly engaged. They can't even administratively or emotionally process the people who have left because of casual indifference or conscious choice for either negative or traumatic reasons. To the shul, they are lost causes.

And then there is my phone—beeping, buzzing, and ringing off the hook. Most of the people who receive my phone number or email address have either already de-shuled, are actively

---

38 Sales, Ben. 2022. "NYC Jews Who Attend Synagogue Have Higher Rates of Emotional Well-Being, Survey Finds." *Jewish Philanthropy,* March 18, 2022. https://ejewishphilanthropy.com/nyc-jews-who-attend-synagogue-have-higher-rates-of-emotional-wellbeing-survey-finds/.

de-shuling, are considering de-shuling, or are surreptitiously going to use me to supplement their synagogue education system that is still falling short of meeting their needs. I wake up every morning in August to similar text messages. "Hi there, I got your name from X, I'm a member of Z congregation, and it's my child Hudson/Zoe/Chloe/Celine/Jayden's mitzvah this year. She/he hasn't learned anything in Hebrew school for the last few years and I wanted to know if you have time in your schedule to take us on, and lead our service. Also, we are thinking about going to Israel (you come with us, right?) or doing a *havdalah* service and then party, and just leaving our synagogue entirely. Also, I have a set of twins that are eight years old and I'd like your advice about when to start them with you. We really just care about the traditions, but want them to be ready for their mitzvahs and also know how to say their *haftorahs* before camp because they go away for the whole summer." I get some variation of this message all year round via email as well. Or, "Hi Rebecca, I heard about you through Jaime/Jamie/Jen/Jennifer/Heather/Holly/Haylie/Hayle/Haily/Aime/Amy/Amie and I'm planning a wedding for a super popular four-day holiday weekend in six months, and I'm looking for a rabbi who I can really connect with to officiate the ceremony. She speaks the world of you. Are you available?" Sometimes I hear something like "Hi Becky! Robin/Robyn/Caren/Karyn/Keren/Laura/Lauren/Lori/Melissa/Marissa and I work together and she told me you're the best. I am looking to convert in time for my wedding to my long-time boyfriend. I was raised as 'X' religion, but don't worry, I am not religious. He's honestly not that religious either but it's really important to him that we raise a family Jewish and he wants me—and I want to do this before the wedding. Can we talk about conversion?" And less common: "Hi rabbi, I'm going to connect you with my dear friend, who's parent is about to pass away. They don't belong to a synagogue but it's really important to them to have a Jewish funeral done by a rabbi and I thought of you. Thanks for taking this client on such short notice."

So, what gives? I have found that Jews still get meaning out of marking big moments in a religious way. On the one hand, religious institutions see a massive decline and yet, I witness Jewish people still have desires to mark their holidays and life cycle moments. They yearn to learn about their traditions and cultures. For many, the station at which they filled up their religious tanks has become out of date and out of touch. I had one client tell me the sheer fact that I texted her a PDF with my rates and terms of service was reason enough to switch away from schooling with her synagogue that only mailed paper copies. Another told me that the synagogue they used to belong to was hypocritical in that it was flexible to allow for same-sex marriages and for electronics on the stage or *bima*, yet it kept to an obscure *halacha,* Jewish law, and restricts blessings over the Torah to only one participant at a time. To this woman, hypocritical observance seemed outrageous and she chose to go elsewhere for her family's membership and children's religious education. No institution should be on that thin of ice—but in reality, people have far less patience and a choice to do literally anything else with their time besides shul. Once you don't keep all the rules (Orthodoxy), the door is open for people to see the hypocrisy. People prefer community, leadership, and communication that fits their lives in *this* century, not in a construct that was developed by old men one-hundred-plus years ago. In fact, in *The Great Dechurching*, the authors interviewed dechurched individuals on their likelihood to return to the church. One out of five respondents said they would return to church if they felt a need for more belonging in their life, and twenty percent of respondents said they would return if they had more inspiring clergy or institutional leaders.[39]

What does this mean? America is not a nation of non-*believers*; it is a nation of non-*participants*. And according to all of my data, it means that Jews are just like everyone else. Americans are absent from institutional attendance but still feel a part of their religious groups. They don't belong to a place of worship but they have a sense of belonging to a faith. America is not G-dless, and in fact, all Americans should be able to find G-d in places outside of the traditional church structure. While anyone who runs a church or temple must feel incredible pressure or mounting doom, for practitioners like me, this information signals hope. People still search for meaning in their lives.

If religious institutions are failing, then what do we do? Drawing from Jewish practice, the first step of coming back from sin is repentance. We must admit and confess our sins, take accountability, and with this introspection, make a plan to do better. This technique is borrowed from my favorite holiday, *Yom Kippur*. On this, the holiest day of the year, the Day of Atonement, we confess our sins in the plural form in two famous texts: the *Vidui* and the *Al Chet*. Some have the custom of beating their hearts when they recite each individual imperfect action. I can remember seeing my older sister, Rachel, sitting next to me in shul, thumping her chest with her fist, and hearing the hollow echo of its impact against her ribcage. Always one of my spiritual role models, I thought: *this girl knows how to repent.* Through the plural grammar, the prayers emphasize that everyone in our community has done *at least* one of these bad deeds. All of us are sinners, messy, subpar, and all of us can do better. I am included in this. I don't bear all the responsibility nor do I have all the answers for why religion has

---

39   Davis, Jim, and Michael Graham, *The Great Dechurching*, 125.

slipped. Yet, I care deeply about getting it back on the right track. We must get over ourselves, out of our own way and get back to the goal. We must reinvigorate our traditions and worship so that participants see them as an energized and meaningful branch within their tree of life. I care profoundly about the continuation of all faiths as a practice. Studies have shown that practitioners of faith have higher mortality rates, and less instances of depression, anxiety, and suicide attempts.[40] The community and purpose religion gives to someone is irreplaceable.

This book will outline strategies both that I've employed with my clients and also share best practices from other religious providers. Why should you care? Because those rates of depression, anxiety, and loneliness are most common amongst Gen Zers, who are the future. What you're about to read are seven case studies with extraordinary families that I worked with to achieve different religious goals. They were all seeking a Jewish experience. For various reasons, they all felt like they needed something outside the box. Maybe it's part of being successful in New York City—no one is cookie-cutter here, so why should formulaic practice work for most people? Shouldn't something as personal as belief and *becoming* be personalized *and* customized? You'll read about each family's mission and how I managed to complete it, sometimes only by the skin of our teeth. I'm a one-woman synagogue/Hebrew school/super Jew/counselor/best friend. I want to share people's journeys with you. As a part of each section, I'll finish with a speech, or *d'var torah,* from the client themselves, reflecting the deep study and evolution they undergo.

Ultimately, we're not just in the post-denominational era of religion. We're in the *Postmates era*: people want what they want,

---

40 Lawrence, Ryan E., Maria A. Oquendo, and Barbara Stanley. 2016. "Religion and Suicide Risk: A Systematic Review." *Archives of Suicide Research* 20 (1). https://doi.org/10.1080/13811118.2015.1004494.

when they want it. Here's my best attempt to deliver. I often get asked how my job works—being a "Jewish life concierge," or being a freelance rabbi, and working with some of the most high-profile families in the world. How soon do I start working with clients or children? Do I have total free rein? Do I work within a synagogue or have the ability to lead services anywhere? There are a lot of questions and oftentimes I don't have all the answers. The landscape of modern religion changes all the time—but I do my best to stay up to date. There is no one-size-fits-all G-d; perhaps that is why the Jewish people have always said that our deity is all powerful yet has no form or shape. Likewise, there should be no one-size-fits-all way to practice, facilitate, or learn.

May you feel inspired by these stories of faith and transformation. May we all feel stronger for what we choose but respect those who choose to believe differently than us. May religion be used to cut a wider and deeper swath across peoples in general to convey positive life values and ideals that are productive for the individual and society at large. May we work to improve the Jewish community and beyond; may we try to improve interfaith relations and strengthen organizations that promote mutual respect and learning amongst all peoples. May we live in a world where we feel our actions speak the truth of our hearts louder than anything else. May peace fill the earth as the waters fill the sea.

Let's get Jewish.

CONFESSION III:
I don't feel the need to go to synagogue.

"The center of Judaism is in the home. In contrast to other religions, it is at home where the essential celebrations and acts of observance take place, rather than in the synagogue or temple. The synagogue is an auxiliary. A Jewish home is where Judaism is at home, where Jewish learning, commitment, sensitivity to values are cultivated and cherished."
—RABBI ABRAHAM HESCHEL

I didn't grow up *that* religious. But even still, the way I *did* grow up is in conflict with the way I live now. On any given weekday in New York City's posh Upper East Side, I can be found with my MacBook Pro and shih-poo, Scout, on my lap. I'm likely sitting in my living room or in the beauty salon. Either Cindy from St. Vincent or Jenny from the Dominican Republic, my friends and go-to hairstylists, add wavy curls to my long brown locks and someone asks me a question about where to find a Jewish holiday calendar online. Both the salon regulars and stylists know me as the young female enterprising rabbi—I guess I leave an impression. Under the din of hairdryers, as my long pink nails clack away at my computer, I hear people getting ready for trips, business meetings, and the like. I'm building custom prayer books, following up on invoices, and emailing with private families that I serve like a Jewish life concierge—a personal rabbi. I smile, thinking how different my rabbinate is from those who taught and trained me.

My outfit is nothing like the frumpy dresses of teachers or ill-fitted suits with wrinkled button up shirts from rolling and unrolling a sleeve to wrap *tefillin*, leather prayer phylacteries, of my bearded male rabbis. Then again, I'm from a different generation.

Let me try to break it down.

I grew up in the idyllic suburbs of Washington DC, in Potomac, Maryland. Past winding tree-lined roads and a one-lane bridge, a half-hour's car ride away was my entire word: The Charles E. Smith Jewish Day School (JDS). It feels like I spent most of my upbringing within the walls of this rigorous and wholesome small private school. While half of the day was spent learning usual general studies like math and language arts, the other half was totally immersed in all things Jewish and taught in the Hebrew language. My siblings and I thrived in the dual-curriculum program and enjoyed studying Torah and other scripture, prayers, Jewish law, and modern Hebrew. I would race to complete the entire school year's new Hebrew grammar workbook within the first or second weeks of classes. I would try to do my older sister's Hebrew homework too. In my spare time, for *fun*, I would make dioramas or computer drawings of Bible stories. In the fifth grade, I took a giant cardboard box, covered it in tin foil on three sides, and cellophane-wrapped over the front to make a cross section of Jonah sitting inside the belly of the whale. I would volunteer to do reports on the weekly Torah portion. I would create quizzes for my classmates and reward those who answered correctly with candy. In high school, I assistant directed the middle school Hebrew musicals. I led daily class prayer *minyan*, a quorum of at least ten Jewish adults for public worship, because I loved to sing and I could *daven*, recite prayers, so efficiently that my peers and I would always have a few free moments for socializing before the first period bell rang. I was a teacher's pet and loved learning.

I trace my value of *Torah lishma*, learning for learning's sake, to my dynamic and brilliant educators at JDS. Many of my favorite teachers were Israeli and some of the most memorable educators had survived the Holocaust. Even if you didn't have a survivor as your teacher, you heard their story. One of the teachers, Mrs. Lowy, had her uniform from Auschwitz displayed in her second-grade classroom. Many of my classmates had grandparents who were survivors. I distinctly remember our annual assemblies on *Yom HaShoah*, Holocaust Memorial Day, during which I cried with my classmates; we heard of the atrocities perpetrated by the Nazis, and I had many friends who mourned losses or imagined the torture of their family members. Some of the teachers' origins were Arab countries from which they were exiled after the establishment of the State of Israel. My sister's fourth grade Hebrew teacher was a lively Yemenite woman, Mrs. Horn. I imagined she got her name because her family always blew the ram's horn at religious holidays in the fall—but I have no idea if that was true. Mrs. Rozmaryn survived the Nazis death marches. Mrs. Etzion was hidden by her father and told us a story about a family jeweled comb that they hid in a floorboard during the war. Respect for the past and Jewish suffering was ingrained in the students. It was normal. Mrs. Kedem, the hardest teacher, made us memorize Torah verses and would bang her hand on the table to get us to be quiet. She was remarkably austere, donning long hair and only black clothing because one of her sons had tragically passed away. Mrs. Lerner, an Israeli educator, was the smartest woman I knew and commanded all of my respect; she was my Hebrew and Torah teacher in third and sixth grade. As I got older, I had wonderful teachers, mostly Israeli women, who taught me modern Hebrew and scripture. My only male teacher was the most special, jovial man named Yoram Bar-Noy; besides being one of our class advisors, Mr. Bar-Noy taught me the stories of Joshua, Samuel, Saul, and David for several years in honors

Bible classes. Mr. Bar-Noy also supervised daily prayer minyan and was one of the first supportive men in my life to recognize my ability to lead services. I looked forward to visiting JDS when I was in college and catching up with my favorite educators. My teachers' integration in my life was contrasted by distance from the headmaster of my school, who was male rabbi. The interim principal during my high school years was also a male rabbi. All of my rabbinics classes were taught by male rabbis. At the many synagogues with which my family maintained memberships, all of the rabbis were men. Therefore, I believed that a rabbi, the figure head and spiritual leader of a community, was a role reserved for men.

To further complicate things, I lived simultaneously in two worlds. I was raised as a devout egalitarian Jew and my family was also modern. We were one of the only families who drove to synagogue on the Sabbath because we lived too far away to walk. As opposed to spending weekends in synagogue youth group, I studied vocal performance at the Washington Conservatory of Music and spent summers at a prestigious performing arts program. I even had a high school job selling clothes at United Colors of Benetton at the Montgomery County Mall about twenty minutes from my house in Bethesda, Maryland. I loved makeup, nail polish, jewelry, and fashion. I played many lead roles in school and community plays. I pushed the envelope with my costumes and makeup. I recall times my Orthodox teachers would express their displeasure at my loudly colored nails, lipstick, dangly chandelier earrings, and extremely high heels. My mother, Merry, who was a Barbie look-alike, was also sometimes ridiculed by school staff or other mothers for wearing sequins, eyeshadow, and bright colors. But we were active members of our synagogue and participants in community Jewish life.

Unlike most of the Netflix series you see about Jews feeling repressed by their religion, renouncing their upbringing, and running away from their insular communities, I loved my very Jewish childhood. Perhaps my enjoyment in my religion was because we were not stringent followers like some of the Jews portrayed on TV. I think I am from a rare breed, especially because Conservative Judaism seems to be dying out. While I knew plenty of people who were Orthodox, we were not. We were a hybrid. I also wasn't the least religious person I knew. While I did have a dress code, I could breathe in my clothes and wear color. In my adult life, I actually dated a *Haredi*, ulta-Orthodox, man whose parents were contacted by his dry cleaner upon receiving his colored shirts; an intervention was held. I didn't grow up in a space like that. My love for Judaism was synonymous with loving life. The only real ways I knew how to express myself was through Jewish channels like prayer, Hebrew music, and poetry. Also, I felt great about my family's roots in Israel.

I often attribute two things to my strong Jewish foundation: being raised in a loving home with joyous Jewish experiences, and a day school education with equal importance on religious *and* secular subjects. My parents have a beautiful and loving marriage, with their engagement story anchored in Jerusalem and my mom's desire to live in Israel. Merry and David Eisenstadt got engaged in Jerusalem and decided to build their family back in the US with one agreement: their children would attend a Jewish day school and speak fluent Hebrew. My older sister, Rachel Leah, younger brother Eli Benjamin, and I are the products of that agreement. In fact, all three of us chose partners that have similar upbringings. A citizen of America and Israel, Merry worked as a journalist for various Jewish press outlets. She wasn't one dimensional. As we played childhood dress-up, my creative mother dolled me up in a pop-star Madonna costume, and would put on the karaoke machine so my sister and I could perform our routines. I had a poster of Paula Abdul hanging in my bedroom until I went off to college.

My mom and dad are incredibly practical people and nurtured my interest in working. My father, Dr. David Eisenstadt, is a PhD economist who taught me early on that I could monetize any skill. As an eleven-year-old, I used to call up babysitting clients and request a higher rate with my father's coaching: "My Saturday night has an opportunity cost." From the Monday after my bat mitzvah, I opened a business and began instructing other children in Hebrew and taught them how to chant from the Jewish scriptures. My parents sometimes drove me to tutoring sessions at other people's homes and allowed me to turn our dining room into my office. By high school, my after-school hours and weekend were split between time at the synagogue, managing clients and students, school work, and rehearsals for various performances.

My childhood *Hazzan*, cantor, was Abraham Lubin, Cantor Emeritus at Congregation Beth El of Montgomery County, Maryland. He trained and encouraged me with his ever-present smile and joyful demeanor. I also discovered I had a way with children who were shy or struggled with the complex Hebrew language. I would specialize with children who had learning disabilities and attention-deficit disorders, which had become increasingly diagnosed. No obstacle was too great to help a family or child achieve a goal. Anyone can learn for a bar or bat mitzvah; one especially meaningful experience was working with a student with a profound developmental disorder. Through a musical and creative service, the family and I were able to craft a meaningful lifecycle event for this enthusiastic boy.

And it's never *too late*; I even teach adults, especially women who never were given the opportunity to have a bat mitzvah when they were of age. (A decade before Zoom was popularized during the pandemic, I taught my own mom Torah cantillation over

Skype sessions.) I have always found a way to excite a family or child about their studies. Maybe a student liked learning about our rich history, current events, or maybe they just love singing prayers. No matter what, religion has so many points of entry.

In my youth I didn't feel my blend of religiousness in tension the way I do now. I didn't get asked constant questions or experience public scrutiny and judgment as I currently encounter. In my early years, I simply followed what my parents and Jewish day school laid out for me. There was a lot of happiness and joy around all of the observance, learning, and teaching. My religious identity was inextricable from enjoyable time with doting grandparents, troves of cousins, community, and the music and prayers we loved to sing. We didn't strictly keep the Sabbath—we marked it with some level of observance. Even though I've played around with varying levels of religiosity, to this day, marking, but not by-the-letter observing, is what still feels the most comfortable for me. Sometimes we'd go to the mall on Saturday after services. When I was little, we always had family dinners with my grandparents on Saturdays at either J.J. Muldoon's or Wu's in Bethesda for Chinese food. We never ate pork, but kept kosher style when dining out. Once I made the choice to keep fully kosher, I would only eat vegetarian food out of the house. Wu's dinners would be the hardest for me, as I began replacing Kung Pao chicken with Kung Pao tofu.

My four grandparents were also quite a mix of religiousness. My mother's parents, the Madways, were a blonde haired, blue-eyed, gentile-passing, and prominent family. The older I get, the more I see how they actually resemble my current clientele. Grandpa Ralph spotted Grandma Bette at a dance hosted by the Penn State Jewish student group, Hillel, and even though he was pinned to another girl, fell in love at first sight and asked my grandmother to dance. Before she would allow him to walk her home,

Bette had asked the Hillel rabbi for his approval of my grandpa's character. Ralph was the youngest of nine siblings, only two of whom were born in the US. A branch of Ralph's mother's family had emigrated to pre-Israel/British Mandate Palestine in the early nineteenth century to escape pogroms and antisemitism in Karlik, Russia (now Ukraine—oy a whole other can of un-kosher worms right there). My close Israeli family members are primarily based in the city of Haifa.

Most of the Madways moved to the Philadelphia area. After attending the Reserve Officers' Training Corps at Penn State and rising to the rank of major in the US Army in World War II in France and Germany, Ralph and two of his brothers, Harry and Sam, expanded their father Rubin's lumber business into sizable real estate development and engineering firms. Siblings Alan Madway and Pauline Madway also played notable roles in the businesses.

Bette and Ralph eloped right before he went to Europe. When Ralph returned, they started on making a family, which grew to four children. The youngest is my mother, Merry Ann. My mother followed through with her own mother's mission to strengthen the ties between the Israeli side of Ralph's family and the American relatives. Merry made her first trip to Israel when she was sixteen years old. When my mom was young, the Madways all belonged to The Main Line Reform Temple of Lower Merion, Pennsylvania, where she eventually married my father.

As a child, I thought the Madways lived completely non-religious lives—especially because my mom didn't have a bat mitzvah. By the time I knew them, my Madway grandparents were de-shuled. For example, when Grandpa Ralph put on a *tallit*, religious prayer shawl, at my sister's bat mitzvah, he unknowingly wrapped it around his neck like a scarf. They always ordered muscles or linguine with clam sauce and I dreaded going to vacation dinners in Atlantic City with them, fearing I would get sprayed with non-kosher shellfish juices. Still, I was always proud of the Madway buildings and real estate legacy. I still meet people who have parents or grandparents that live in my grandfather's buildings in the Main Line. In fact, by sheer coincidence, I officiated a wedding for a very special bride, Ali Cohen, who married an equally wonderful groom, Joe Kroll. (Their exuberant wedding was held the first weekend after October 7th, with special mention of our joy in the face of threats and destruction.) While working together we discovered that the bride's grandmother lived in the Madway's Greenhill building after Grandma Bette brokered the sale of their family home. My mom said Bette was the queen of real estate. For me, Bette was an amazing listener and great pen pal. She was supportive when one of my cousins started their gender-transition therapies and surgeries for reassignment. Bette used to keep samples of makeup from the Clinique counter that my sister and I loved to use. She gave me a bag of junk costume jewelry and upon going through it I noticed it actually contained some real fourteen karat gold pieces. From that bag, I wear a charm on my necklace every day; the charm is her name, BETTE, vertically cut in gold, with a little diamond at the top. The Madways were modern, glamorous, secular, and open-minded, yet somewhat formal.

On the other hand, my father's parents, Jack and Revelyn Eisenstadt, were warm, traditional, and modest. They were the dictionary definition of Jewish grandparents. They slept in the same full-size bed their entire marriage of over sixty years. Down-to-earth memories include Jell-O molds, hand-shaken milkshakes, art projects like collages made out of spare buttons, dinners consisting of meatloaf, presents wrapped in repurposed news-paper comics, games of Go Fish played with a pair of ice tongs in a bucket of pennies and, of course, stickball. The Eisenstadts lived in the same house for close to fifty years until Jack's advancing dementia forced them to downsize. They belonged to their Silver Spring Conservative-movement synagogue, Ohr Kodesh Congregation, since its founding. They celebrated all the Jewish holidays, and came to all the performances and sports games of their ten grandchildren. As a sergeant in the US Army, Pacific Ocean theater, during WWII, Grandpa Jack worked as a cartographer for the US Defense Mapping Agency. Grandma Rev had worked first in the Nestlé chocolate factory in upstate New York, then as a governess in Washington, DC, and after as an administrator and secretary for agencies in Washington, DC. But she really excelled as a visual artist. Grandma Rev was the oldest girl of her seven siblings, and my dad always said she was the smartest.

The Eisenstadts spent nearly every weekend with us as a family. We shared synagogue services, Saturday night dinners, trips to the public pool, Grandma Rev's personalized art classes, and eating baked potatoes at fast food restaurants. Even when Grandpa Jack's Alzheimer's disease caused him to lose all speech and ambulatory skills, he would still hum the tune to the *Chatzi Kaddish* prayer as he was wheeled through the hallways of his nursing home. Jack and Rev were my parents' best friends, and my greatest influence other than my parents. I could talk to my grandmother about everything and shared my deepest feelings with her. As I got older and she prepared to live in an apartment, I enjoyed long visits sorting through her decades of possessions and hearing about family history. Grandma used to wear rings that seemingly cut off the circulation in her meaty fingers. Their Silver Spring house was robbed in the nineties and most of Grandma's fine jewelry was stolen. I don't believe she had that much to steal, but luckily, whatever she had left in terms of fancy jewelry was just what she wore daily. She wore a ring that was made up of the birthstones of her three children and small diamonds from her mother, Rose Bernstein-Kamp. My aunt, Susan Eisenstadt Drei-fuss, who is now the matriarch of our clan since Revelyn passed, made a ring for my sister, my cousin Jessica, and myself out of those stones. Since 2008, I have never taken off my Grandma Rev ring with two diamonds from my great-grandmother and the ruby symbolizing my father's July birth date (my siblings and I were also all born in July).

Besides schooling and family, there are many wonderful summer camps that reinforce Jewish values, learning prayers, and foster friendships that last a lifetime. Indeed, camp and Jewish lifecycle experiences seem to be the only joyful Jewish moments Americans can agree about. The future of religious education may very well be in their combination. Unlike where most of my Jewish day school friends spent their summers, I went to a few summer programs. I always felt a little sad that I didn't go to one of the many religious camps like Camp Ramah. While my grandparents summered in the Catskills, my father had attended Camp Kaufmann. My mom went to Akiba and Camp Shalom, among others; those various Union for Reform Judaism programs fostered her Jewish foundation. At ten years old, I started going to a predominantly Jewish camp, Camp Louise, that had limited Jewish content in the Catoctin Mountains in Cascade, Maryland. However, the camp felt extremely non-religious in comparison with the rest of my religious upbringing.

After my bat mitzvah, I really took womanhood seriously. I also wanted to start my training as a professional actress. I had done research about camps that would be a great launch pad for my budding talent and help me make it as an entertainer one day. The all-girls Belvoir Terrace Performing Arts Program seemed like a good compromise, situated in the idyllic Berkshire Hills of western Massachusetts but centered around many cultural insti-tutions like Jacob's Pillow and the Tanglewood Music Center.

The other camps were coed and my parents were too conservative to send me away to both a secular camp *and* a coed overnight camp. I remember my phone interview with the owner. She said something to the effect of: "Yes, most of the girls here are Jewish, but are you sure you wouldn't be happier at one of those *Jewish* camps?" I was determined to go, and it was more about convincing my parents.

Perhaps I should have listened to the owner's advice. It was on the first day, after I unpacked bags, set up my bed and said a tearful goodbye to my parents, that the campers loaded into a large dining hall for lunch. "Kielbasa" was written on a chalkboard and before that day, I had never heard that word. I asked a girl next to me what that was and she told me it was pig hotdogs. My mouth must have dropped. Stunned, I asked, "Aren't most of the girls here from New York? Aren't most people here Jewish?"

"I'm from *Manhattan*," she corrected me, as if that was the answer to her place of origin and religion. I had never been in a place where Jews openly ate pork. That day I decided I would never eat non-kosher meat again and never have.

Later that same afternoon, I actually experienced antisemitism for the first time. I was excited to wear an asymmetrical one-strapped leotard for dance class. Always modest and uncomfortable getting undressed in front of total strangers, I got dressed under my comforter on my top bunk. Feeling proud of my costume change, my mood quickly changed when I was suddenly accosted by a strawberry-blonde-haired girl who resembled a Barbie doll. This physically beautiful teen popped off her bunk bed and said, "I know why you're wearing that leotard—you're *Jewish* and you're too cheap to afford the other strap." I was speechless—I knew there were people out there that believed Jews were greedy and cheap; but where I came from Jews were generous and behaved like everyone else. I certainly wouldn't have thought of *us* as cheap—frugal or smart with spending was something else. Immediately I felt like an *"other,"* and that consciousness has never left me. Still, none of this was enough to deter me from my inner-pride for my Jewishness. If anything, this was all part of some heavenly plan to draw me to meld my two worlds.

(As an interesting aside, decades later, I was called by the now director of the same camp to teach her child for her bat mitzvah and supplement her Hebrew tutoring. We maintained a relationship mostly because my brother had gone to the brother camp, Greylock, and was a superstar camper and athlete. I visited the camp as an adult to teach that student. I helped this child, also in high school, write an essay for her biblical literature class. When I told the camp director and her daughter these two stories, they were horrified and apologetic. I told them it helped shape my identity in positive ways.)

After moving out of Maryland, I made my way to Manhattan to study at New York University's acclaimed Tisch School of The Arts, with a minor in marketing at the Stern School of Business. I wanted to be a performer and producer. There, I began to see where my natural talents were most appreciated and in conflict. I was appreciated for my ability to do voices and characters (a natural talent I can attribute to having so many Eastern European or Israeli teachers and family members). I had a deep sense of history and intellect that informed my performances and personality. While well praised and highly graded for my talents, my marks were threatened by unexcused absences for religiously observed holidays and even the Sabbath. I couldn't attend Friday night services at the NYU Bronfman Center because my rigorous program had classes until 6:30 p.m. on Fridays and often the Sabbath would start well before then. I couldn't attend important auditions at the start of the year that conflicted with Yom Kippur. No one in the acting program wanted to eat with me in the kosher dining hall. I had to navigate my Jewish observance with eating and personal identity. I decided I would join the student senate and form a religiously sensitive club that produced plays with all-female casts.

It was in my third year at NYU that I met my mentor, the prolific composer, director, and writer Elizabeth Swados. Swados found me in my formative years and shaped the woman I am today. She was most famous for her groundbreaking Broadway musical *Runaways*. By the time she was twenty-eight years old, Liz Swados had four Tony Award nominations, an Obie (Off-Broadway's highest honor), and countless other awards. Liz Swados was a part-time faculty member at the Tisch School of the Arts. For one of the mainstage productions, she was going to rewrite and devise an adaptation of the Yiddish Classic *The Dybbuk*. As Liz had a commanding presence and reputation, I was nervous but determined to try out. In my audition, I had to make an otherworldly sound and I screamed from deep within my *kishkes* (guts). I didn't know Liz at all, but after I let out the shriek, I saw her light up and her eyes pulse. She pulled me aside at the callback and immediately told me she cast me as the lead, the girl who gets possessed and eventually exorcized. Liz trusted me during the process to guide the cast with Jewish dramaturgy, authenticity, and even religious instruction. When technical rehearsals geared up toward the weeks of production and overlapped with the holy days of Passover, Liz told me I shouldn't travel home to Maryland for first and second seder meals. Instead, Liz gave me her credit card and let me organize and cook a kosher seder meal for our cast and crew of forty people in her massive New York City downtown loft. We went around the table reading from xeroxed copies of various *Haggdot*, seder scripts, singing and explaining to a group of mostly non-Jewish, and definitely secular, college kids about the iconic Exodus story and freedom.

With Liz, I expected to star in many future productions.

Instead, she asked me to manage literary works for her. At first, I was disappointed but I soon understood her plan. Liz wanted to groom me as a writer, collaborator, and content creator. She and I worked on many musical and literary projects, often with Jewish subject matter. In our meetings on the soft blue couches, we talked for hours about dating, gossip, and my supplemental work as a Jewish educator and tutor in beautiful New York homes and iconic houses of worship. That we were both Jewish, had wild, long hair, and loved shopping, was only part of our similarities. We found inspiration in our teaching, meaning in mentoring others, and both cared about making money, though I was much more business minded. Liz helped me see that I could have an impact outside from being an artist. Liz kept telling me I was too smart to just be an actress, and yet, when I would just focus on teaching, she did not want me to give up entirely on art. She loved the duality in me and memorialized it in some of her writings. She had hundreds of poems that remain unpublished, some that feature me with soulful cole-lined eyes, sentimentally worn down with a charm necklace, kicking the dust with cowboy boots, and long hair like hers whipping in the wind. As gifts, she let me keep the handwritten copies once I decoded and transcribed her shaky handwriting that often had no vowels.

"You better be writing all this down," Liz would instruct during our long meetings in her Mercer Street loft. It was always the same greeting; I'd buzz her from downstairs and she'd let me in saying "hellooooooo." I'd take the large clunky elevator up to her second-floor apartment, and as soon as the chrome elevator doors would open, I'd see Mz. Liz standing in her doorway, waiting for me with a smile. Her thick maroon mane would be pressed against the doorpost and wisp up towards her stone *mezuzah* (doorpost accessory containing a piece of parchment inscribed with verses from the Torah) that was designed by her friend, artist

Tobi Kahn. Wearing comfortable and warm boots, long baggy pants, and a tighter shirt, Liz was always dressed in layers, as if it were cold outside. Her thin, lanky frame led me slowly into her playground for artists and creativity; her bed was more of a jungle gym with a custom slide, stairs, and even poles to slide down. The floor would always creak under our feet and I would feel honored thinking of all the luminaries who had stepped inside this apartment before me: Joseph Papp, Elie Wiesel, and Julie Taymor. Past the piano, African drums and dolls, posters and awards, beyond the modern but mostly unused kitchen and steel counters with pill boxes filled for each day of the week, we'd sit down in the center, on the mismatched ink-stained, dog-chewed blue couches. They were set up in a square formation for salon-style conversation. Curious trinkets from Liz's various travels and books were stacked everywhere: poetry, history, graphic novels, and a space for notebooks, reading glasses, pens, and sheet music yet to be written. It was always too warm and my black clothes would turn even more black around my abdomen and arms as I'd sweat during our lengthy talks about all things: literary and poetry work, chasing grants, discussing politics and ideas for new plays or musicals, THE JEWS, my failed dating life, and gossip. I would tell her stories about breaking through to young children on the Upper East Side and accessing their spirituality; it would remind her of the work she did with runaway homeless youth, or relationship building in Washington Heights between Hispanics and religious Jews. Maybe due to her own complicated upbringing with mental illness effecting family members, and ultimately her mother dying by suicide before she was twenty years old, Liz understood young people in their quest to find themselves. She never judged a struggle with darkness but was a torchbearer to help you out of your own tunnel through the other side. Between stories about the actresses Liz had helped to launch (Meryl Streep,

Diane Lane, Shaina Taub, and more), Mz. Liz would insist that I wait to settle down and marry; I should break free from religious norms. Liz wanted me to be a leader in the Jewish world.

Like Liz, my mother and father started to suggest a career change to Jewish clergy, but it took me years to warm up to the idea. I did not believe a woman could really hold any such title. Plus, while I was already a "Jewtor," a religious tutor, since the age of thirteen, I wasn't totally ready to let go of being an artist. Moreover, I was afraid of what others would think of me becoming a female rabbi. I doubted if I was even legitimate as a clergy member, as only modern streams of Judaism accept female rabbis.

One of my favorite projects Liz and I worked on was an oratorio about Rosh Hashanah and Yom Kippur called *Atonement*. Then, at age nineteen, famed Tony-winning Broadway composer and actress Shaina Taub was our musical director. Tony Nominees Grace McLean and Justin Levine were in the cast. Years later Liz also composed the music to my lyrics of a musical about the biblical sisters Rachel and Leah. But Liz's health was up and down, with public struggles with bipolar disorder, and later, a gruesome battle with esophageal cancer. I continued to assist Liz, and worked as a Jewish lay leader; I avoided more serious rabbinic training. I stayed hanging in the balance.

I worked as a Hebrew school teacher, professional Torah reader, family religious service facilitator, bar and bat mitzvah tutor, Hebrew tutor, math tutor, translator, Yiddish actress, Jewish musician and performer, and graphic designer for more than a decade after college. I had a free membership to gyms by working for SoulCycle. I would write, audition, teach, date, fail, and try. I would go to Israel every chance I could. I read books and newspapers in Hebrew. I lived with my older sister. I was diagnosed with Celiac disease in 2011 after being extremely anemic, vitamin deficient, and ill. I was overextended, tired, and unsure of what would bring me a fuller and more steady life. I always had a different Jewish boyfriend—whether Israeli, Sephardic, Persian, or Ashkenazi. Nothing was really working for me. Then Liz got cancer.

One of the last times Liz actively guided the course of my life was through her last work. *Walking the Dog*, a novel published by Feminist Press, was released after Liz tragically passed away in 2016. I remember when she began to write it and told me that she was including me as a character. Elisheva is me: an enterprising b'nai-mitzvah educator who wears dark eyeliner, performs in Yiddish plays, spins while wearing a heavy charm necklace, and helps the main character mend relationships through Jewish lifecycle moments. In the last scene of the book, my character leads services as a rabbi. At some point during the writing process, Liz sent me a draft and asked me for notes. In the hospital, while working on the book and reviewing Elisheva's character arch, I asked Liz if that was what she wanted for me. Liz nodded. She wanted me to start the process for formal cantorial or rabbinic ordination. There was an urgency in us both, as illness reveals how fleeting life and time can feel. It was the push I needed to break free from what held me back and take the lead. I'm lucky that my visionary mentor honestly told me exactly how she envisioned my life working out. I was allowed to change course midstream and that encouraged me to open my tightly held fists to swim a different stroke as the tides changed. Liz believed in me more than I believed in myself. She knew me better than I knew myself. She had been on earth longer than me and seen that change is possible and necessary. I was allowed to redefine my relationship to my religion and its leadership without being disrespectful. She understood that I didn't have to be one thing, and that I could be a trailblazer like her. I was allowed to ask for a seat at the table even if I didn't resemble the others already with a place setting. I should trust where I came from, my deeply Jewish foundation, all of the work we did together, and my strongly developed inner voice to guide me for the future's tough choices. Liz used to call me the "Jewish Wonder Woman," and reminded me that I possessed all the skills of teaching, storytelling, leading, singing, and empathy to be the title of rabbi— which means "master." It was *kosher* to let the gentle current of the universe and her guidance support me on my journey. I started interviewing at religious seminaries right then and began my quest to become a rabbi.

The biggest obstacle I had to overcome was my own fear. I held misconceptions about the few female rabbis I knew. I worried about how others would judge me. Now, I constantly hear people say, "You don't look like any rabbi I've ever known!" I experience a mix of imposter syndrome and butt up against my own and others' old-school thinking. This critique, at times, has shaken me off my game. However, with age and success comes *boldness*. I've learned that you can never make everyone happy. Once I learned to let go, I was able to gain confidence that allowed me to support and lead families—in short to do the real work. For all the people struggling to find their path and who they are: the most important thing is to live authentically and tune out the bull-plop. I take strength in two quotes: one from Jeremiah 1:18, and the other from an original Bravo Real Housewife of NYC. Jeremiah prophesied, "Today I have made you a fortified city, an iron pillar and a bronze wall to stand against the whole land." I protect my spirit and values like an iron-clad fortress. The beauty and strength of my belief, conviction, and personal practice can fortify me against negativity from outsiders and within myself. And, to quote one of my favorite reality TV stars, authors, and business moguls, Bethenny Frankel, who popularized the term "zero fucks" so epically it launched a successful apparel line: "The zero fucks lifestyle is a way of life."[41] I am who I am and I'm proud of it. I drink añejo tequila on the rocks. I keep kosher. I'm head over heels for my dog. I love to dance and sing. I get fired up when I see Jewish people have little to no education. I work out like crazy and even joke that I was even one of SoulCycle's first brunette employees (when I worked there all the girls at the desk were blonde). I am in love with my husband who does more good in the world than most rabbis, but he doesn't feel drawn to religious observance. I long to be a mother but fear how it will impact the rigorous work schedule I keep. I am who I *am*.

I've dabbled in the many sects of Judaism and never felt at home in any of them; from Orthodoxy—with a short stint in the Hasidic world—Conservative, and Reform. A little bit like Goldilocks, nothing quite seemed right. So, like many other seekers, I felt the need in New York City to keep tight to my beliefs and individual practice without ever really finding my own community. I think labels are really useful for other people to define you from the outside, but don't quite do the job of describing a whole person. My husband, Ben, is actually very similar to me. He grew up in Melbourne, Australia and went to a variety of Jewish schools including a cultural Yiddish elementary school called Sholem Aleichem and a Hasidic high school called Yeshiva College Melbourne. He's been involved in the religious and secular Jewish worlds. He is only really drawn to practices that help preserve or elevate the dignity of other human beings. He also has a killer sense of humor and loves Jewish and Russian food. We maintain an active membership at The Carlebach Shul (Orthodox) and are "friend members" at Romemu (Jewish Renewal Movement) on the Upper West Side; still, we only attend our shuls for major

41 Frankel, Bethenny (@bethennyfrankel). 2022. "The zero fucks lifestyle is the way of life..." Instagram video, July 7, 2022. https://www.instagram.com/p/CiV7XONgFSz/.

holidays and frequently visit other synagogues for work and religious events in our community of friends and family.

Years ago, before my husband and I officially started dating, he asked me to have a drink at Bemelmans Bar in the Carlyle Hotel on the Upper East Side. There, the walls are gold, the ceilings are low, and the lighting is warm; I was convinced this was a date. I had just come out of a relationship with someone who was very religious. Ben and I spoke for at least a half hour about the book *Rebbe,* by Joseph Telushkin, profiling the life and work of Rabbi Menachem Mendel Schneerson. We both loved the book, the Rebbe as an inspirational figure, and found many inspiring lessons throughout. Telushkin masterfully tells the story of this seventh-generation head rabbi of the Lubovich movement who transformed Orthodoxy to include loving-kindness, education, race relations, international aid, Zionism, science, and tireless outreach. As the world's best-known Hasidic movement, Chabad-Lubavich is particularly celebrated for their joyful strategies of engagement and welcoming. The term ChaBaD, coined by founder Alter Rebbe Shneur Zalman in 1775, is actually an acronym for *chochmeh* (wisdom), *bina* (understanding), and *da'at* (knowledge)—the top three devine emanations in the *Kabbalah.* The Chabad-Lubovich observances are very close to traditional Orthodox, but culturally the members have differences. Chabad has a pay-as-you-go system which makes it hard to track membership but is attractive to people of varying commitment levels. Pew reports sixteen percent of US Jews participate in some part of Chabad services or programming.[42] You have probably seen their black-hat-wearing *shluchim,* or emissaries, on streets and in parks handing out religious items and insisting Jewish people to say prayers. Chabad is utterly accepting of all Jews—so long as you

---

42   Pew Research Center, "Jewish Americans in 2020," 70. 42

have a Jewish mother. They meet you at basic levels. They have ways for Jews to get involved as little or as much as they want. While Chabad has had tremendous success in their programing, and I have personally benefited from meals and several holidays and Shabbat services at their facilities around the world, they are still Orthodox and geared towards male participation and commandment obligations. For a modern family in the modern world, the way the *Chabadniks,* members, dress can feel strange or off-putting. Due to modesty rules, the large size of families, and limited integration in popular culture, most ultra-Orthodox Jews don't live lavishly, so their lifestyles aren't particularly aspirational for outsiders.

In some ways, my life would have been so much easier if I could have just accepted the life of an ultra-Orthodox community member. I would have gotten married at around twenty years old, had children, and could even be planning my daughter's wedding by now. I had moments in my twenties and thirties that I tried dating ultra-Orthodox men only because I figured after a few dates they'd be crazy not to propose to me. But I was really just trying to put a square peg in a round challah tray. I'm a free spirit and modern person. While sometimes wearing long skirts, I felt ashamed or guilty as a woman who enjoyed wearing pants both literally, religiously, and even for business. I loved to sing at synagogue services while growing up, but I felt silenced during Orthodox services—*Kol Isha* is the well-known prohibition for a man to hear a woman singing, or that woman's voice is not permitted to be heard singing in public.[43] I couldn't stand being on the other side of *mechitza*, a divider, while men would lead prayers; often I was more capable than the Torah reader who

---

43   Hasida, Rav. Gemara Brachot 24a:17 based on Shir HaShirim. (2:14) https://www.sefaria.org/Berakhot.24a.17?lang=bi

chanted with several mistakes and needed corrections. Still, out of respect, when I go to an Orthodox shul as a visitor, I have no problem abiding by their customs. After many months, when I dug deep and checked in with myself, Orthodoxy didn't feel like home to me and that is why I'm not very active in the Chabad communities around where I live.

The problem with Chabad taking over the bulk of outreach to unaffiliated Jews is that the way they *observe* isn't comfortable for a lot of people they *serve*. At some point, those participants hit a wall and will likely leave. Still, the facilitators of Chabad centers have gotten something right and in my exposure to them; I've tried to emulate their openness, friendliness, and non-judgmental nature. They don't try to focus on all 613 commandments but just a few important ones and they build upon them. My core important principles are Jewish education, holiday observance, and literacy.

I call myself "hipsterdox": strict about some things, while cool and flexible about other doctrine. I wish I could take credit for the cute term, but it originated from a strictly observant ex-boyfriend (he loved wordplay more than he wanted to accept and marry me). I won't mention his name, out of respect for his privacy, as not all of his family members even know that he dated someone as hipsterdox as me. Likewise, I started to realize there were many other interesting, successful people out there, who wanted religion in their lives, but they too didn't feel turned on by the current institutional offering. Being de-shuled doesn't mean having left the religion. Nothing compares to the ideal Jewish environment that I grew up in. Maybe I'm nostalgic for time with my grandparents and my carefree childhood eating butter pound cake at the shul *kiddush*, lunch after Sabbath services. After all, I enjoyed going to bar mitzvahs in seventh grade so much that I chose a career with the same weekly itinerary. Maybe it's a combination of a bunch of things that make me not want to go to synagogue that often; but obviously I'm Jewish and I consider myself an active practicing Jew through and through.

To my surprise, I have always been met with more support than criticism. Other than my Orthodox brother-in-law telling me it was social suicide to become a female rabbi, most people think it's really interesting, cool, and important work. All the time, women tell me how inspired they are by my choice to break into a male-dominated profession—it has even gotten me attention from Oscar-winning Hollywood moguls and producers. As it often goes, I was always my biggest critic. It was hard to lean in and I stayed away until I couldn't help it any longer. I can still come up with a thousand excuses why breaking the traditional synagogue model and sharing this book could cause me trouble. There will always be naysayers, "negative Nancys," or people trying to kill the vibe. They cling to the past or resist change that this world so badly needs. Some lead with closed fists and hearts; some govern with fear and exclusion. There will always be a place for purists, but there is a growing need for innovative providers and leaders like me for the future of faith movements.

Like it or not, all religions evolve and traditions change. This is especially true with Judaism, a religion which originally prescribed worship as ritual animal sacrifice in one central temple. Observance and stringency are changing. Because as of 2023, there are just about 15.5 million Jews out there,[44] I feel that we can't afford to lose a single one due to apathy or disinterest. Religion is either becoming totally irrelevant or what you make of it; we are shifting to on-demand mediums in every form of consumerism . . . and religion is not immune to this trend. A lot can be learned

---

44   The Jewish Agency for Israel. 2023. "Jewish Population Rises to 15.7 Million Worldwide in 2023." The Jewish Agency for Israel. September 15, 2023. https://www.jewishagency.org/jewish-population-rises-to-15-7-million-worldwide-in-2023/.

from success stories that follow this model, like Uber, Netflix, Amazon, and DoorDash. I operate my rabbinate similarly. Instead of abiding by an institutional board and organizational red tape, I'm free to work when and how I choose. I'm governed by my religion as I understand it, strong morals, and my client's needs. At one point, I caught the eye of Hollywood producers and made a deal with Reese Witherspoon's Hello Sunshine to develop a documentary series about my professional and social lives as a woman working in a traditionally male-dominated world. It was going to follow the novel work I do and the way I do it. Ironically, we were pitching the show to many of the on-demand streaming networks.

How do I manage to toe the line between modern and traditional, hip and serious, *by the book* but with my own flavor of *chutzpah*? I meet families in their environment, see where they are at, and where they are looking to go with respect to their religious practice. Usually, I come in for a specific moment—like a birth, coming of age, weddings, and even death. I do my best to maintain a relationship and presence after the occasion. These are huge life-cycle moments, but also religious matters. People feel the weight of tradition and G-d when they observe these tremendous markers of time. Why does someone like me particularly *thrive* in this work? I am modern and I look like everyone else who is getting coffee, beauty treatments, or shopping in the same neighborhood. I am open and open-minded. I keep religion relevant and accessible. I've practiced a wide array of observance through the years so I can fit in with almost anyone on the religious spectrum. Because I'm in their home, I'm the whole family's friend or an honorary family member. I'm sure of it, because clients keep inviting me into their homes for the next child's education, more events, holidays, and sometimes on their vacations to Israel. It takes a village and I'm there to help raise their children with values and meaningful experiences.

Rabbis often use stories and parables in their sermons. Normally they access the canon of rabbinic *mashal*, stories that expand upon the biblical stories or Jewish law in order to illustrate a point (like an allegory). As a modern, pop-culturally attuned millennial, I'm going to reference a great story told by the wildly successful comedian, Steve Harvey. Harvey was a guest on episode seventy-eight of the *Shay Shay Podcast* that premiered on April 24, 2023, hosted by three-time Super Bowl champion Shannon Sharpe.[45] As Sharpe interviewed Harvey about his career in comedy and television, Sharpe asked why Harvey never made the crossover into the movie business. Harvey didn't directly answer the question, and instead recounted a night out with Denzel Washington. The two were having dinner at Sweet Georgia Brown in Los Angeles when Washington pointed out to Harvey: "I'm going to show you the difference between me and you. Want to know the difference between me and you? I'm a movie star and you're a TV star," he said. "Watch this. Stay with me. People would come up to me and say, '*Oh My G-d, Mr. Washington, OH MY G-D, Mr. Washington! I watch every movie! I go everywhere! Thank you so much because it's so great.*' You know why man? Because to come see me, you gotta get a babysitter, get your car, stand in line, buy a ticket, stand in another line, buy your popcorn and stuff, go to a seat and wait, and I come up on a screen twenty-five feet tall. Then they leave and they don't see me no more unless they come to another movie. I'm a movie star," Washington said. "Watch how they come up to you. When they know you. As soon as they see you: '*Steve! Whaaaaat! What's up! Hey man! Steve remember that time!?*'" And as Harvey looked at him Washington continued,

---

45 Shannon Sharpe, Steve Harvey. 2023. EP. 78: *Steve Harvey on Divorces, Showering In Bathrooms, Importance Of Women & Daughter Lori. Club Shay Shay.* https://www.youtube.com/watch?v=SEUlZVBP-j8.

"You see the difference? The difference is—I'm a *movie star* and you're a *TV star*. They gotta pay to come to see me and they invite you into their house every day."

Both of these entertainers have become household names with huge followings. But as Washington points out, only one of them feels like family. One of them has fully integrated into the people's lives, by nature of being in their homes all the time, on-demand, and on a regular schedule with weekly TV shows. The movie star exudes respect and awe, but keeps his audience at a considerable distance. Such is the difference between institutional clergy and an in-home and on-demand religious provider. What makes people feel like religion is truly part of their lives will be a provider like Harvey, someone with whom they can be themselves. I often found that the most active members in any synagogue community growing up, including my parents and grandparents, were friends with their synagogue rabbi. (Funny story, the first love letter I ever wrote was to my grandparent's rabbi when I was three years old.) My family found a way to bring the institution close to them. It is hard, but doable. However, synagogues are merging to economically survive rising costs of rent and labor. It is understandably difficult for providers to have enough time and bandwidth for hundreds of congregants and really maintain genuine friendships with all of them.

To demonstrate, I recall the hours before one Jewish New Year began. To maintain anonymity, the following is a composite depiction of real clients stories. Typically, most rabbis with a pulpit or synagogue are putting the finishing touches on their sermons and ironing their formal white robes they will wear the next few days. Not me. I had just returned from a *shiva* call for one of my past clients. If you don't know, after the funeral, the immediate family of mourners sits at home and hosts prayer groups for seven days, otherwise known as a period of shiva. It is customary for friends and community members to stop by, pay respects, and participate in the prayer groups. I was at this shiva to support my former student. Here I am changing their family name and some details out of sensitivity, but those won't effect the moral and purpose of sharing this story. My student had tragically lost his mother. I taught Max Leib from the age of ten until his bar mitzvah. For the entirety of our lessons, my apartment was only four blocks away. I ran into Max's mother practically every day while walking my dog. She was the most loving, warm, and personable woman. She somehow made time for everyone and everything. The Leibs have one other young son that kept up with regular Hebrew school at their synagogue, but Max wanted to work with me for a variety of reasons. Once I finished teaching Max, I also taught his cousins after meeting his Aunt Janet at someone else's pool in the Hamptons. I heard from Janet that Max's mom was ill with breast cancer. In the summer of 2023, I bumped into the whole extended family at Georgica Beach in the East Hamptons when my fiancé and I took a quiet stroll. I noticed that Mrs. Leib wasn't there and asked others how she was feeling. Then, I learned from Max's Instagram account that his loving mother passed away, three days short of *Rosh Hashannah*. I no longer teach this client, nor his family. They don't keep me on some type of retainer or pay me dues. But from our time together, and friendship through study and experience, I am a part of their lives and they are a part of mine. I reached out instantly and texted condolences to all of the family contacts I had. I actually had a death in my own family so I couldn't attend Mrs. Leib's funeral. My mom's Israeli cousin (who now lives in New Jersey) Issac "Yitzchaki" Zaksenberg, lost his loving wife of thirty-four years to ovarian cancer. I remember being a child when Yitzchaki and Beth used to visit our house even before they were married. I remember their wedding was the first I ever attended and I met all my Israeli relatives for the first time in one place. My grandfather's cousin, Rakhel, gave me a box of chocolates that I savored. I loved Beth and have always loved my cousin Yitzchaki, so without question I rushed to New Jersey and represented my family at the modest graveside funeral. Meanwhile, the following day, I did have a chance to attend the Leib's shiva. Shiva is typically held in the home of the deceased; it is said that the soul of the departed hovers close to where they dwelled, and so you sit for seven days on low stools, cover mirrors, wear torn cloth, and *feel* the grief. When shiva coincides with a holiday it is cut short, so there were only two days of shiva for both families. Unlike how the Zaksenberg family held a shiva at their suburban home for my cousin Beth, the Leib's shiva was held in an historic NYC country club with waiters, catered platters, and a full bar even at noon. This is just how shiva works in New York within some circles. It didn't take away, though, from the sadness that there are now kids without their mother and a husband without his wife. I showed up because of the little comfort I felt that I could provide hours before my own holiday, with all the preparations I still need to accomplish. It is one of the greatest mitzvahs, or commands, to offer condolences, a shoulder, or support to the bereaved. However, I didn't see their synagogue rabbis at the country club. This family pays thousands of dollars a year in membership, Hebrew schooling, and ticket fees. I'm sure the rabbis were getting ready for their main event—the High Holidays; that's what those rabbis get paid the big bucks to do. I was at shiva because I'm on demand for people and in their lives when it counts. I didn't stay for the whole shiva, but long enough to give each person a hug and offer support.

CONFESSION IV:
I think converts who meaningfully switch to Judaism are more dedicated to their new religious identity than many people who were simply born Jewish.

Case Study 1

At 8:30 p.m. on October 30, 2015, I received the type of email that is only sent from a CEO.

"R—can you do a couple of hours a week?"

I had never corresponded with this individual. Before just sending the message to spam, I Googled the email address. I realized the email came from the president and CEO of the world's largest independently-owned public relations firm. I knew I had a small connection to him, so I responded with my phone number saying he was welcome to call me. A woman with a Spanish-sounding name was CCed on the email. I made no assumptions. A few short email exchanges later, they asked me to come for two hours every Sunday morning at 7:30 a.m., right after sunrise yoga private sessions, to instruct two adults and two children on "how to *be* Jewish."

The following week, I knocked on the door, not entirely sure I was in the right place. They hadn't yet confirmed if I was going to Riverside Boulevard or Riverside Drive. The address on Riverside Boulevard was a rental building and I guessed these were the type of people who would likely own their dwelling. So, there I was on Riverside Drive, knocking on a door that did not have a mezuzah on it. I was confused, tired, cold, and armed with colored pencils, Hebrew materials, chocolate for bribes, and a charged iPad. Oh, and my bag was full of gluten-free snacks as I had a full schedule—thirteen straight hours of stacked tutoring appointments after that one.

A tall, slender, eleven-year-old boy answered the door. He said something to me in Spanish and then closed the door. I nearly turned for the elevator, thinking I was in the wrong place. Then, the most beautiful, tall woman opened the door. She moved with grand and elegant motions like she was ballroom dancing. Imagine a cross between both the looks and personality of Pené-lope Cruz and Sofía Vergara. "Rrrrrrrebecca! Gooooooooooood morrrrrrrrning! Cappuccino? Latte? What can I get you? We just finished yoga, but we are serving coffees now."

My eyes adjusted to the light of the apartment with wide windows and a perfect view of the Hudson River. I had no doubt she was the woman of the house: Claudia. This had to be her son. The man who had emailed me was nowhere in sight—I had Googled him, so I was aware of his general appearance. There was a housekeeper around, but she moved about her work without drawing attention to herself. In many ways, this first meet and greet was totally unique. Normally, I'm not as fuzzy on who is who when I show up to meet a new client. I am typically greeted by a thin mother, a barking dog, and the potential student on the Upper East Side. They usually have met me before in some way, like having seen me at one of their friend's services. Sometimes the child is a little shy. But the child always speaks English and has no problem communicating their needs.

Here, the boy joined me at the large wooden dining table. He pointed at himself and in imperfect English introduced himself as "Joshua." From the kitchen, Claudia was relaying that first, I would teach Joshua and Claudia in a group lesson, and next Tamara, her younger daughter, would learn with Richard's sister Renée—who was about sixty years of age. It was as if they expected me to know everything about them without any information.

Joshua asked me what his Hebrew name was. I tried to communicate that it was likely Joshua, but I motioned like I was holding a baby and with my broken Spanish said: "Ocho dia—bebe—seyama—Joshua." In my mind I said that he would have gotten his Hebrew name as an eight-day-old baby, when he had his ritual circumcision or *Brit Milah*. It's a pretty hard thing to mime to a prepubescent boy you barely know. Claudia brought me black coffee, bursting out. "Ah no! We are not Jewish. You will teach us how to be!"

I started putting things together. Richard, the CEO, was dating this gracious not-yet-Jewish Mexican woman. I'd learn later that Claudia had worked with the United Nations and Unicef. Besides being stunning, she was strong, brilliant, eloquent, and vivacious. I'd discovered she was the daughter of a famous Mexican actress, Cecilia Romo. Claudia Romo-Gonzalez was divorced and had many interesting prior boyfriends. Now she was seriously dating Richard Edelman. He was also divorced and Claudia was bringing a whole new flavor to his otherwise corporate life. Richard was her companion and was helping her children to adjust to life in New York City (while having three accomplished older daughters from his previous marriage).

Claudia was eager to convert her family to Judaism in time for her son to become a bar mitzvah in 2016. Many Orthodox rabbis had already turned her away. Claudia had fallen in love with the spiritual congregation, Romemu, on the Upper West Side. She joined and enrolled her children in their Hebrew school. The synagogue, however, had guidelines for what a bar mitzvah would need to accomplish, along with attendance expectations, and not a lot of flexibility for a child who needed to catch up or have a lot of hands-on explanations. I deeply admire all of the clergy who work there, especially Rabbi David Ingber, Romemu's founder and figure head. But like most synagogues, Romemu has grown so large that individual attention to each member is impossible—especially when a family needs a lot of hand-holding. Richard and Claudia knew they were a special case and were grasping to find someone who understood their commitment and passion. She had a date for the bar mitzvah celebration and a goal in sight. Still, Joshua (eleven years old) and Tamara (ten years old) barely spoke English, and hardly recognized a single Hebrew letter or Jewish tradition.

I felt their ambition to study, learn, and live as Jews. This wasn't a simple hour-a-week tutoring gig. I had to ingrain *Jewish Literacy*[46] into each family member's brains, and *fast*. I knew that I was the only one who would and could take on such a complicated mix. Wakeup at dawn on Sunday mornings. Conjoined lessons for mother and son. More conjoined lessons for a mismatched child (ten years old) and sort-of-step-aunt (sixty years old). I'd have to balance appointments between language tutors, private yoga, sports teams, and jet-setting. I'd have to teach slowly and with visual aids until the children's English would improve enough since my Spanish wouldn't catch up. From letters aleph-to-tav, Torah stories, and Jewish holidays, I was on call—teaching the family as a unit. I watched them compete, laugh, learn, and connect to the way they longed for their whole lives. I helped them learn how to make it click, unlocking the language, the prayers, and meaning behind the mysterious religion they sought to participate in.

On Sunday mornings I'd show up, Claudia and Richard would be finishing their yoga. Joshua was always wearing his flannel pajama bottoms with his 9/11 museum T-shirt (Richard handled the public relations for the memorial museum.) Joshua would still

---

46 Telushkin, Joseph. 2008. *Jewish Literacy Revised Ed: The Most Important Things to Know About the Jewish Religion, Its People, and Its History*. William Morrow, an imprint of HarperCollins Publishers, Inc.

have sleep in his eyes, and required not only cereal, but way more review than Claudia. Half-focused, Claudia would go back and forth from the kitchen to the dining room. I'd watch the most adorable mother/son bonding you'd ever see. The sense of competition between mother and son would wake Joshua up. They would race to read, answer my questions, cross out words the other was reading so they could mess the other up. It was silly and cute. We ended up working at warp speed because of this sense of competition. Claudia's razor-sharp intellect pulled Joshua into adulthood, but the silliness of her son allowed for Claudia to enjoy our learning. We got Joshua and Claudia reading in Hebrew within a few weeks.

With Tamara, lessons were a little different. Renée would get such a kick out of letting Tamara do all the work, reading, singing, and learning. Sometimes I would think she was a doting aunt, and other times I would think Renée didn't want to focus that early in the morning. The more I got to know Renée, the more I learned just how much she desired to one day have her own bat mitzvah in Israel, but struggled with reading Hebrew in public. Consistency wasn't her strong suit. Renée is not only a great friend, but one of the most loyal and thoughtful people in New York. She loved her brother dearly. Richard wanted Renée to get to know Claudia but it was also extremely important to Renée to be a part of her brother's exciting new life. As a cohort, Renée learned the letters and vowels, but Tamara learned to read faster. They became mismatched not just in age but also in goals. Frequently my two hours with the Romo-Gonzalez-Gisiger-Edelmans were more like one hour with just Joshua, thirty minutes with Tamara, and another thirty minutes with whichever adult was focused enough to work with me.

Any and all combinations were okay with me. Each week we'd make progress in our reading; first we'd review the letters and vowels we already knew and add one or two more letters and vowels in order of the Behrman House suite of books that I had come to prefer. We'd play games like Hebrew tic-tac-toe and or matching games that I would create beforehand. We would have timed reading exercises that mom and son would compare times for motivation and compete against each other. We would, as a family, gather around the table with my iPad and watch bible cartoons or stories about holidays. Normally, I'd find the content prior to a lesson on YouTube from a Jewish provider or even Christian cartoon creators. After all, the stories are all the same.

I rarely had to check in with their synagogue to let them know about Joshua's progress. I knew what the end goal was: a bar mitzvah consisting of at least one Torah *aliyah,* or section of the Five Books of Moses, certain prayers, and a deep and reflective speech. Claudia and Richard were my bosses, not the synagogue. Yet, plaguing my mind, since meeting him, was Joshua's circumcision. I had taught other male converts, all of whom had already had a physical circumcision as a baby, so any conversion would not include a surgery. But as Joshua was European and Mexican— he was uncircumcised. As his date for conversion approached, his circumcision was looming. I felt bad for him. I didn't really think this happy-go-lucky, tall boy with clumsy limbs knew about the physical pain in-store. I don't remember all the details, but I know the procedure was scheduled a few weeks before he became a bar mitzvah. He couldn't play basketball for two weeks and missed school for several days. I remember he was on acetaminophen with codeine, and when I tried to teach him for a few lessons he was still healing, so it was hard for him to sit still. With years of perspective, I wonder: *did he really know what he was committing to? Did he want this? What did his Swiss, non-Jewish father think?* I never asked him and I feel bad looking back. To me, the procedure was non-negotiable if he was to convert to Judaism. In 2015, I thought Joshua had to be circumcised to show his emotional and physical commitment to G-d—I had taught him the *Shema* and *V'ahavta* prayers, "You shall love G-d with all your heart, with all your soul, and with all of your might." This was the epitome of enacting that commitment and performing that commandment as he set out on his Jewish adulthood. He completed it. G-d bless him. If he is truly now a New York Jew (especially of Gen Z), he'll probably undergo some period of psychoanalysis later in life. I hope whatever trauma he unpacks will help him make sense of it all. I cannot imagine a twelve-year-old boy undergoing such pain in such a developing area of his body as part of his religious *belonging* ceremony. I hope he can reflect favorably upon this choice he made with his mother. I hope that the physical pain or its eventual unpacking will not estrange him from Judaism itself.

Joshua converted on January 15, 2016, on a cold winter Friday before marking becoming a bar mitzvah. As Claudia was also studying, her conversion was completed later on June 16, 2016. Even though the dates were five months apart, in my fond memories, it's as if the events happened on the same day. I was the first to arrive at the modest unmarked *mikvah*, ritual bathhouse, building on the Upper West Side. I went inside and another conversion group was gathered with my friend Rabbi Mira Rivera, the first Filipina-American woman to be ordained at The Jewish Theological Seminary. I decided to wait outside to give Mira's group space. Everyone was running late, including the Romemu founding rabbi who eventually rolled up via bicycle. Joshua, Tamara, Claudia, and her larger-than-life mother, Cecilia, all poured out of a yellow cab, dressed to the nines. I couldn't tell if I was asked to be there as a teacher, facilitator, babysitter, or personal concierge. As I was not yet a rabbi, I was not part of the tribunal of rabbis to sign the certificate of conversion for mother and son. An associate young rabbi joined our group in jeans and a low-cut T-shirt and I thought to myself: *no—this isn't the right vibe.* My Modern Orthodox sister was a member of the same mikvah and I accompanied her there before her wedding day. It was the first time since I went back to the townhouse. I felt like we were in a scene of *The House of Bernarda Alba*, a 1945 play by Frederico García Lorca which documents a mourning period in deep Spanish-Catholic tradition. I observed Claudia as deeply somber and defiant like one of the Alba daughters. Claudia understood the gravity of what was in front of her; she was to leave behind the house of her mother and father. Unlike the play, Claudia's mother, Cecilia, was jubilant for her daughter's new sense of purpose and peace.

We gathered in a ten by ten-foot room with uncomfortable, narrow chairs. The ceilings were low and we had many coats and bags. It was early in the morning and Tamara and Joshua had to go to school after the family became Jewish. The mikvah lady instructed Claudia to remove all of her nail polish and makeup before submerging. She nodded, recognizing the instructions. She had read them one hundred times on Wikipedia and in manuals about conversion. Rabbi Dianne Kohler-Esses, the first Syrian-Jewish woman to become a rabbi, joined our group; the kids recognized the brilliant and warm rabbi from their Hebrew schooling. Rabbi David arrived donning a bike helmet, khakis, and a button-down. He explained quickly to Joshua where to undress and how to dunk in the ritual bath. The procedure: The person converting will completely undress and shower first in a holding room. They even floss their teeth and file their nails. Enveloped in a robe or towel, they will knock to enter the room with a ritual bath, then immerse their body fully, say a blessing, then immerse fully two more times. Joshua seemed excited to just cannonball into a warm bath. I waited and kept Tamara company with her grandmother. Cecilia sang songs while Tamara played with her hair and my hair and asked me questions. The other smaller conversion group finished and they wished us good luck and *mazal tov,* congratulations. I was also checking my cell phone for two reasons: one, I had to go to work at my Broadway producing job, and two, I wanted to see if I had any messages from Richard. When would he arrive to mark the transition of his bride-to-be as a new Jew? Finally, he whirled in like a businessman ready to start a meeting, likely leaving his wool cashmere overcoat with his driver in the town car. He checked his cell phone for emails while on a conference call. He had the air of "this will only take ten minutes, *right?*"

Soon, Claudia and Joshua both emerged from the spa locker rooms in white robes with wet hair. Joshua looked as innocent and floppy as a wet puppy. Claudia looked like a glistening goddess. Her shining shoulders were square and straight. Her hair dripped heavy with holy water ringlets. I was in awe of how she carried with her the weight of the moment, the crown of her new Hebrew name—*Malkah Ruth*—Queen Ruth. The rabbis handled the moment perfectly. They drew us into a circle and enclosed Claudia and Joshua. Rabbi David placed a large white prayer shawl over both of them and instructed them to cover their eyes. Instinctively they sang the holy words of the Shema: "Hear oh Israel, Adonai is our G-d, Adonai is one." Claudia sang loud and tears streamed from under her hands. I felt a magnetic pull from her mother near me, who was proud, weeping, and giggling. We bursted out into a circle and whirled around the mother and son. The horah dance ended and the three rabbis signed their two conversion certificates.

The three rabbis stayed on the sidewalk and I continued traveling four blocks south to a fancy restaurant with the family to have brunch. The clergy went about their day via their bikes and subway. I joined the family for an efficient breakfast celebration, only having two lattes but enjoying the friendship and my place at the table. I was also going to see them later that night, at their

Riverside Drive apartment, as we welcomed in the Sabbath and had a family meal together.

Joshua's bar mitzvah ceremony was the next day. His Torah portion was about stepping into the leadership role despite the fear and doubt Moses felt when G-d first called upon him. At his service, he gave a rousing d'var Torah that turned into a pep talk to his congregation. His message was to "be a Moses" with courage and to take a stand against the injustice of Pharaoh. He gave his speech entirely in English. He sang his prayers beautifully in Hebrew. Romemu required students to lead many parts of the service besides a few lines of Torah and he worked tirelessly to learn prayers that most children would otherwise know through the osmosis of being Jewish. He stood tall and confident. He thanked his mother and Richard for their love, care, and for helping him learn (and pushing him in school and basketball). There was not a dry eye in the congregation. I sat in the front row, with water and a second copy of all of his materials like a stage mom. I must have been mouthing the words he spoke. We danced around him and continued the afternoon service. The family had arranged a long luncheon celebration at a nearby restaurant. I was exhausted from the emotion. I remember bonding with their friends and family from all over the world, making new connections for new clients. Mostly I was so glad my involvement with the family was not over. I knew I was going to continue to work with Tamara and Renée.

I linked the family to the touring company they used on their family trip to Israel. That included celebrating Hanukkah in Jerusalem. It overlapped with one of my trips to lead someone else's mitzvahs, so I was there too, in the same hotels. One breakfast, Claudia found me at the King David Hotel in Jerusalem, and told me Richard might propose to her. I even helped them look for a diamond. The enthralled couple celebrated their Jewish wedding in September of 2017. I had the honor of helping them plan their Jewish ceremony and I said one of the Hebrew blessings under the wedding canopy. Rabbi David Ingber officiated the religious ceremony in their home. The next day, in the Hamptons, they had a secular wedding officiated by Reverend Jesse L. Jackson. The married couple joined the board of their synagogue, on which they serve to this day.

The CEO, who was Jewish from birth, had not just facilitated his new wife's transformation but something in him changed in the years since I have known him. He had three daughters from another marriage with a woman who also converted. With respect to religion, much of his prior life was passive and color-less. However, Richard is one of the smartest, charming, and connected men I've ever met. He seemed to be a man with tremen-dous manners, dignity, and class—but someone who was slightly asleep until Claudia. When he met Claudia, he opened himself to criticism, deep feeling, and vibrance. She painted their dining room orange! More than that, he allowed himself to connect to G-d by bringing her into *his* culture. Also, Richard didn't want to go on the journey alone. He wanted to bring his side of the family into it too; I perceived that since his daughters were at first distant, he invited his sister, Renée, to join us for weekly sessions. In an atmosphere of learning together (and under the umbrella of "it's all for the children"), Renée was able to unite Richard's former life with his new life. When we started working, Renée had been dealing with a cancer scare. Reintroducing Jewish life was also Richard's way of giving his sister a sense of faith. Renée has oodles of good friends, but no children of her own. Renée is an even more active member of her conservative synagogue and continued to study with me long after Joshua and Tamara were finished.

Once Richard and Claudia were married, Richard's three

daughters started to integrate with Claudia's two children. Claudia's daughter, Tamara, was a dream student. She was adorable, motivated, loving, graceful, and gifted as a vocalist. Tamara was one of the most loving children I have ever encountered. She had so much empathy for me when my mentor, Liz Swados, passed away. She would always bring me back a small gift from their exotic travels. She was responsible and kind. She loved my dog, Scout. She was easily everyone's favorite in the family. With my own penchant for drama and fairytales, I questioned why I had yet to meet Richard's daughters. But when it was time to plan Tamara's bat mitzvah ceremony for the fall of 2018, it was important to Richard for at least one of his daughters to participate in a large way.

Tamara's conversion was far less painful, as it just required a dunk in the ceremonial mikvah. I remember dancing and singing with grandmother Cecilia who had come again from Mexico to celebrate in the Upper West Side ritual bathhouse waiting room. Tamara sang the most beautiful *Shema Yisrael*, "Hear O Israel," with a prayer shawl over her head. I can still see her long straight hair dripping with pure water. I felt so confident that this girl was destined to be a Jew and share her love of G-d with others. It didn't matter if she were Catholic, Jewish, or any other world religion; Tamara used prayer as a way to express her inner beauty and it was as pure as a pearl. For her upcoming prayer service, Tamara prepared with me and her cantor, Hazzan Basya Schechter, a rock-star Jewish musician and religious facilitator I've admired for decades. Basya and I had a Liz Swados connection, a Yiddish Theater commonality, and a compatibility in both being performers. Basya graciously collaborated and instructed me how to help Tamara shine.

Much like her mother in the United Nations, Tamara was great at bringing people together. Tamara had asked her youngest stepsister to learn an aliyah. This is considered a tremendous honor. It was also a way for Tamara to involve her sister and split her spotlight. Most twelve-year-old girls don't want to share any of their big day, but Tamara was gracious. Yet, I felt the stepsister was reluctant and kept postponing lessons with me. A week or so before the bat mitzvah I caught her on the phone for a practice and she was not just underprepared; she barely knew a thing. She was going to embarrass herself and her father. I gave her what my mentor called a "verbal spanking." *Did she not understand the gravity of being called to read Torah? What about the significance of being honored like a sibling? Was she really going to stand up in front of a congregation and signal to her stepsister that she couldn't care less?* So often what makes me the provider that people prefer is that I know exactly how to cut through bullshit excuses when it counts. I said something that conveyed: "These people matter. You may not have to work that hard at many things since you are naturally brilliant. But you have to work hard at relationships, and I expect you to do it for Tamara." She spent another forty minutes or so on the phone with me and did a much better job.

Tamara's bat mitzvah was one of the most emotional days of my life. It was the final service for which the family needed me. Romemu held services in a church in Harlem. As a modest congregation made up of spiritual and down to earth people, the sanctuary is both humble and G-dly. I arrived very early and rehearsed Tamara and all the participants while we tested microphones and took photos. Rabbi David Ingber came in later and took over and I knew to take my seat in the first row, as a private tutor, not working with the synagogue, but as part of the *family*. Claudia was also reading Torah for the first time and gave a deep speech about being a woman of faith. Joshua had an aliyah, now standing a foot taller and chanting confidently. Richard read

Torah, and as an honored member of their community, I recited the blessing before his reading. When it was time for Richard's daughter to chant from the Torah, she fumbled only a few times through her section. She stepped up and tried. She set an example for her other sisters that they would have to bring open hearts and effort to make their new family work. That was a real *mitzvah*. The Catholic family from Mexico had all traveled to witness this tremendous moment in time and brought so much positivity and cheer. Grandmother Cecilia would be one of the many to tragically pass away in the first months of the COVID-19 outbreak in Mexico.

The enormity of my role on this day hit me: a girl with a Mexican mother, a Swiss father, and an internationally celebrated Jewish stepfather, became a bat mitzvah. Tamara Sofia Valentina Romo-Gonzales-Gisiger, chanted Hebrew from the Five Books of Moses, delivered a heartfelt speech, and was blessed by her community and mother, Claudia Romo-Edelman. Tamara was destined to follow in her mother's size-ten footsteps as a multilingual powerhouse, with beauty inside and out. During the entire service, I stood by Tamara's side as her trusted teacher and friend. In order to convert to Judaism, I taught Tamara and her whole family. Our years of study flashed before my eyes: from nearly the moment they arrived in the US and moved in with Claudia's successful then-fiancé, they studied how to be Jewish, and passed with flying colors. Claudia had been seeking meaning and purpose for decades. Tamara's bat mitzvah was the culmination of the entire family finding that sense of belonging with G-d and religious community. It was one of the most uplifting services of my personal and professional life.

Elated from my student's accomplishments, I took time exiting the rickety synagogue space. If you've ever been to a shul, then you know how there is a lot of socializing after services. The modest *oneg*, celebratory lunch, was a vegetarian potluck. Children and families feasted on braided challah bread, grape juice, carrot sticks, hummus, and fruit platters. I was still sweaty from nervous perspiration during the service and my thick stockings were tight around my legs and waist. I didn't want to leave the warm building, but felt physically uncomfortable. I said my hellos and goodbyes and knew I'd see everyone at the party that night at a nightclub downtown.

When I finally turned on my cell phone (use of technology is not permitted inside Jewish places of worship on the Sabbath), to my horror, Twitter and Apple notifications alerted me of terrible breaking news. There had been a deadly shooting at the Tree of Life Congregation synagogue in Pittsburgh. The worst hate crime perpetrated against Jewish people ever in the US had just happened. With my nose in my phone, I frantically jumped into the first yellow cab I could find and called my mother—a former investigative journalist for various Jewish press outlets. First, I let her know I was okay. Then we debriefed on the grim details of the unfolding crime scene in disbelief. My grandmother, Bette Davis Madway(z"l), was from the same Pittsburgh suburbs. I had gone from a super high to a terrible low in a matter of moments. At a shul with similar liberal values, not unlike the one I was at, eleven Jews were gunned down in cold blood.

It was that weekend that I would feel a fire to finish my rabbinic degree and ordination fast. I had trouble focusing on anything else for the rest of that Saturday. It felt strange going to Tamara's celebration party and not getting right to work. I didn't dance other than the obligatory horah. Tamara had all of her international guests parade around with the flags of their country. She asked me to represent Israel since we were there together. I was draped in an Israeli flag that on the one hand felt like a sash of pride and on the other like a target. I drank tequila and seltzer by the bar and I remember an older guest was hitting on me. I could barely stay past 10 p.m. The day was endless.

The next day was a typical Sunday full of appointments with other *Jewdents,* what I call Jewish students. I remember sitting on the floor in a beautiful Park Avenue apartment with a boy named Jake, who's bar mitzvah was going to be the following weekend. Even though the Pittsburg shooter had been caught, and Jake's New York synagogue had security with metal detectors and armed police stationed in front at all hours, Jake was afraid of copycat attacks. With the Tree of Life attack, Jake had discovered that antisemitism still existed. His bubble burst. He had naively thought Jew hate was in the past, not since WWII. Now, he was afraid for himself and his family to host his service in one of the largest synagogues in New York City. The family didn't call the congregation's senior rabbi for reassurance, it was me, their private educator, coach, and trusted Jewish life coordinator to have the final lesson and guide this distressed boy through his emotions. He got up there the next weekend and did great. While I was in the congregation cheering him on, I sat with his cousins and siblings, all of whom I also taught. I wondered if his synagogue's clergy really understood how much of a struggle this was for him only a week before. I wondered if they really saw him, knew him and his family, or if he was just the fourth kid that weekend having just become a bar mitzvah.

Beyond his fears, I heard a calling louder than ever: to serve niche families that have needs beyond the typical walls of the synagogue. Maybe they don't fit the traditional mold of what a classic Jewish family used to look like. Maybe they require additional hand-holding. Maybe it is a combination of the two. Over and over, in my professional life as a tutor and teacher, I had noticed a need not being met by traditional providers and people feeling put off, disenchanted, or ostracized by their synagogue. Yet, the desire to still have Jewish experiences and lifecycle moments never leaves these people. So, I vowed to become a rabbi but within reach. I would not work with a pulpit but with people who need me and seek me out. I have found ways to bring people and families closer to their culture and spirituality goals. I felt Rabbi Hillel's talmudic teaching driving me: "If not now, when?"[47] I vowed I would step up in a bigger way as a leader. I would help even more people have access to our Jewish customs and grow into the title of "rabbi": master teacher and of religious facilitatior. I would not stop bringing customs, faith, and G-d, even in the face of violence. The worst hate crime against Jewish people perpetrated on American soil simply because of Jewish identity occurred on the day I swore again to become a rabbi. I was ordained less than two years later from the same seminary where the rabbi from the Tree of Life Congregation obtained his rabbinic ordination.

Claudia's Conversion Essay

"Do not urge me to leave you, to turn back and not follow you. For wherever you go, I will go; wherever you lodge, I will lodge; your people shall be my people, and your G-d my G-d."
—BOOK OF RUTH 1:16-21

I am becoming a Jew on June 16, 2016. My conversion has been one of the most important journeys in my adulthood through which a lot of my character has been built by testing the limits of my perseverance and conviction.

It struck me all of a sudden, more than twenty years ago, that I belonged to the Jewish community. I was in Israel, though not at

---

47 Hillel. "Pirkei Avot, 1:14." Sefariah. https://www.sefaria.org/Pirkei_Avot.1.14?lang=bi

one of the many holy sites in the country. I was in a meeting with a group of technology entrepreneurs when I had this moment in which I simply knew that I found my place.

I was raised in Mexico in a very religious country within a very spiritual family. But as grateful as I am for my deep sense of faith and for everything I gained from Catholicism, it was not the final destination for me. Since very early on I was seeking the right hub that would allow me to expand into my spirituality and at the same time exercise my intellectual curiosity. I was eager to find a place where I can question and debate the meaning of every single word and at the same time get lost in praying and inner reflection.

Ironically, there it was, in a technology meeting, loud and clear, this inner voice speaking to me. I still remember the warmth and intense satisfaction I felt once I found my new fate. I was probably the only person in that room that had a spiritual revelation by having a discussion about trends in technology.

My sense of warmth and desire to be Jewish was tested many times through many years. I knocked many times on different doors and tried different ways. I knew that I wanted to be part of what I saw on the other side, but every door seemed to be locked. For years, maybe a decade, there were ups and downs; I felt rejected, questioned, and laughed at. Yet, at times I would be embraced by people that opened their hearts and homes to welcome me, and then my children to experience the Jewish life and holidays.

At some point, adversity makes you resilient. I became even stronger in my conviction. I decided to give my children distinctively Hebrew names, Joshua and Tamara, today twelve- and ten-years-old, to make a point and to allow them to have an easier entry to their Jewish life.

I hardly spoke to them or anybody about the joys and pains of this journey. Today, I just want them to know that it is worth *fighting for what you believe deep in your heart to be your truth. To become Jewish is to be true to myself. It is the longest fight I have ever engaged in. I am clear that every single tear, every time I felt laughed at, every time someone discouraged me to continue, was worth it. I found the place where I belong, my community, that today is walking next to me—helping me to cross the door and become formally part of the Jewish family.*

From the first day I came to Romemu, I felt the power of belonging, of community, of being part of a greater family that cares for each other and for the bigger world. I am deeply grateful for my rabbis who have been inspirational and embracing to me as a woman but also to us as a family. In Romemu people are free and expressive—they sing, dance, meditate, hug each other, and show their vulnerability.

I am also deeply grateful to Richard, who is the only person that has treated me as a Jew for years, no questions asked, and has been my biggest supporter in this process. May G-d bless you, Richard, and get you closer to freedom and expression.

Today is the beginning of a new life and I welcome it. But I also recognize that there are some things that I leave behind and that I need to mourn adequately as I lose them for life. As a child, one of my favorite celebrations was Christmas, particularly the Christmas tree. I loved everything about the tree—the smell of pine, the process of decorating it, the memory of my cousins and I dancing and running around it, the men discussing politics, the women chatting in the kitchen, the presents. But my most fond memory was that moment in which the lights were plugged and the entire tree was illuminated. Today I know that by becoming Jewish, I will not have a Christmas tree again. And those sensations will not be passed to my children or my grandchildren. I don't want to pretend it doesn't mean anything. Maybe at the end of year I will mourn it and miss it.

I am choosing Judaism with eyes wide open knowing that there are gains and losses. Part of what I am gaining today are new names. My Hebrew name is Malkah Ruth. Daughter of Abraham and Sarah.

Malkah, a queen, a place I know well and where I feel at peace. Either professionally or personally, I have very often in my life been in a queen position, always at the right side of the king, the leader, the commander. I was the eldest daughter of a very dominant man and very early in my life recognized that the best place was not necessarily under his wings but next to him as counselor. My mother gave me the other side of the coin of being a Malkah—a royal training. I learned from her a life example of what it means to be a queen—contended, decent, elegant, generous, and strong at all times; even in the darkest of the moments, of which she had plenty, starting with the loss of her two young babies when she was only twenty-five years old.

Choosing the name of Ruth is also very significant. The Book of Ruth was recorded by the prophet Samuel. We read the Book of Ruth on Shavuot for two reasons: First, because Shavuot is a harvest festival and the Book of Ruth gives us a picture of the harvest, and how the poor were treated in the harvest season with sympathy and love. Secondly, because Shavuot is the anniversary of the passing of King David, who was the great-grandson of Ruth and Boaz, whose story is told in the Book of Ruth.

But perhaps the main reason is because it gives us such a vivid picture of the ger tzedek, true proselyte. Shavuot is the "time of the giving of our Torah," and when we received it, we too, like the ger tzedek, pledged to accept the Torah and fulfill its 613 commandments. I see so many similarities between Ruth and myself and aspire to become a ger tzadika as well. I have challenged my own history and destiny, just like Ruth. She was not born an Israelite, was a single mother, she was not accepted and was called a foreigner. She chose to stay and embrace Judaism as her religion, her family, her lodge, and her destiny. And she became the great-grandmother of David, King of the Jews. The Talmud calls her Ima Shel Malchut, Mother of royalty. My name is Malkah Ruth, Queen Ruth.

Sarah was also not born Israelite and was given a new name to enter the covenant when she was Sarai. I got a new name to enter the covenant and be part of the Jewish people and this community. Just like Abraham and Sarah, today in receiving my new Hebrew names, I vow to G-d and to the community to be loyal to Judaism. That covenant that started by Abraham, I will pass down to my children and that be passed forward. I am entering the covenant today.

Today is the beginning of my new Jewish life. I always felt Jewish, but now I am acting Jewish. The possibilities are huge. I can only imagine the family traditions and new life that we will explore and adopt. Only last year I have been studying Hebrew on Sundays with Rebecca Keren, learning songs, debating traditions at Monday class, hosted my first ever Passover, and will only continue to learn and grow. G-d willing, our family will travel to Israel, now with the new perspective of leading a Jewish life.

Just like the decoration of a Christmas tree—I have been preparing and decorating myself with new traditions and beliefs to embrace a Jewish life. Now is the time to plug the lights in me that drove me and attracted me so much as a kid. Today, the lights connect me to my internal and eternal light. My conversion to Judaism is lighting my ner tamid and everlasting Jewish spark.

My takeaways from working with the Romo-Edelmans run deep. I am grateful to them for entrusting me with so many aspects of their Jewish education and experiences. I'm grateful to the

Romemu community, Hazzan Basya Schechter, and Rabbi David Ingber for allowing an outside educator to work with their congregants. Obviously, I didn't detract from their commitment to Romemu. I even joined Romemu due to my enjoyment of their community. I have brought other families in as members as well. The Romo-Edelman modern family—international, multilingual, high-achieving, and made up of many religions, is an example for how we can all come together in support of one another. I was so inspired by Claudia's passion and determination to lead her family. I was moved by her mother's support. I was heartened by the love that Claudia and Richard found and nurtured later in life. It's all possible. I am struck that these huge moments in this family's life included religion and their close relationship to religious teachers. Rabbis and religion give life's moments structure. We are close enough to advise and distant enough to actually command respect. Religion and religious providers can unite people from different backgrounds. All of the above serves as a reminder: religion *can* and *does* bring deeper meaning into people's lives. This is why I am now a Rabbi.

CONFESSION V:
As Jews, we have a lot of anxiety and real enemies.

Case Study 2 (Names have been changed and identities have been obscured or written as a composite characters)

I met the Weiser family through their Synagogue rabbi, David Gelfand, of Temple Israel of the City of New York on the Upper East Side. He had seen the way I worked with other families as a private educator and on-call Jewish big sister. He recognized that I never infringed upon a family's larger commitment to their home-base synagogue. Temple Israel's building was in need of a facelift to keep competitive with other beautiful Reform congregations (and maybe even congregants). Rabbi David knew I could help prominent donor families while keeping them engaged. Although I wasn't a member of Temple Israel (and therefore I didn't report to Rabbi David), we had a great working relationship. He had built a following—first out in the Jewish Center of the Hamptons and then continued to build up one of the biggest Reform synagogues in Manhattan. Rabbi David is a man with bright white hair, tanned skin, big lips, and big hands. In his office are crowded, messy shelves with scores of books, but not just *seforim* (strictly religious texts). He seems to know something about everything, which makes him apt to serve educated New Yorkers. I still have a copy of a book he gave me, *Thou Shalt Innovate*, by Avi Jorisch. The book is about how even a small country like Israel can be full of technological advancement, mostly due to the Jewish value of constant improvement and reinvention. Rabbi David told me he was going to send my contact information along to another family.

Tali Weiser, a chic and sharp woman, called me and asked me if I had Sundays at 3 p.m. free to work with her eleven-year-old son, Jack. While she was from Sephardic Jewish descent, her husband was Ashkenazi; they were raising their four boys in the typical Reform Jewish style. Jack seemed to be falling behind in Hebrew school. There was no real reason she could pinpoint, but I suspected it was just the usual: classes were only once a week after long days of school which resulted in behavioral problems amongst a class of fifteen ten-year-olds. Couple that with educators who are only moderately committed to their part time jobs, with little qualification or training. They end up spending more time disciplining than creatively teaching. If participants miss even one session, they are confused and either check out or act out. For my first one-on-one session with Jack, I did what I always do. I was prepared with a brand-new Hebrew workbook, an iPad, colored pencils, candy, and a clean slate.

I met Jack in one of the most beautiful town houses I've ever been in, right on Fifth Avenue. Everything was ivory, stone, and pristine. There was still construction blue tape holding brown paper over certain surfaces that were brand new. The family was renovating a multilevel apartment building and turning it into a mansion. Two grand iron doors, led into a sprawling foyer that had one of those curling staircases you see in prom photos. I was used to those in houses in Maryland, but not in New York. On the wall hung a large Jackson Pollock painting. I only expected to see that artist's work in galleries or museums. Tali greeted me in the marble hallway, along with several staff members who instructed me where to back up and place my shoes and coat. We would have our lesson in the tutoring office room that doubled as the shoe closet for the adults. This closet and office was nearly the size of my apartment bedroom. It would be years before I'd get a full tour of the house.

With shaggy yellow hair and tilted eyes, Jack looked like a cherub. My mom was blonde too, so I was used to blonde Jews. Still, I instantly thought about how *goyish,* or "non-Jewish" my Eisenstadt grandparents would have said this all felt: uniformed staff in a palace—having a lesson like I was "the help" in a shoe closet. I wondered: *who puts the Jewish educator in a room like that?* If one of my teachers had come to our house, they would have gotten the red carpet. Then again, there was no carpet here—only ivory imported marble.

I told Jack we could start from the beginning and we did. Our trust and friendship grew. I realized he seemed really anxious about all things Hebrew even though he loved being Jewish. To him, being Jewish was something he could never fail at, because he knew he had Jewish blood, history, and background. He was a natural at world history and possessed a detailed memory for stories. However, he struggled with remembering the different Hebrew characters and sounding out words. He was not disciplined enough to practice. While making Shabbat blessings over the candles, wine, and bread was routine for the family, other than holidays, they did not attend synagogue. For Jack, what took some students a month to master took him longer. Still, he was my favorite male student. He tried so hard and was so respectful. His parents were lovely and communicative too, just very distant.

As our lessons continued, I wrote quarterly progress reports to the synagogue religious school about what I had taught Jack. From the same spreadsheet recounting session lesson plans, I duplicated another copy and created invoices for Jack's family to pay me. I emailed the invoice and the father's personal assistant transferred the balance directly to my bank account—sometimes even the same business day. I always communicated progress this way. I sometimes felt tension as a supplementary tutor having to report to the director of a supplementary school, explaining that this student still needed so much additional work to grasp what his educators should have been able to accomplish during Hebrew school. Even if Jack needed a little extra help, he shouldn't have been so confused and lost.

Years ago, I worked as a Hebrew school educator at Congregation Habonim on the Upper West Side. Before the school year, educators had mandatory training sessions and workshops, led by Rabbi Laurie Phillips (z"l). Rabbi LP gave me a copy of the book *Teaching Jewishly* by Joel L. Grishaver. On the back cover, an endorsement from Dr. Gail Dorph, Director, Mandel Teacher Educator Institute reads: "As teachers we know that students learn not only from what we teach but from how we teach and from who we are as we teach. Grishaver's new book teaches us ways in which the 'how' and the 'who' can be deeply infused with Jewish ideas and values . . ."[48] The exercises we utilized from that book as well as the workshops stayed with me and set the general tone of my teaching. I taught second and fourth grade classes. No amount of money was worth the frustration I faced with kids of all different levels and attendance track records trying to learn letters and build upon concepts. Students' behavior at the end of the day was understandably atrocious. When I would complain to parents with behavioral reports there were always excuses or explanations, and I felt increasingly mean while working there. I hated going to work and dreaded the two days a week I had those classes. I still enjoyed coleading Tot-Shabbat services for families with babies and toddlers. I admired and respected the

---

48   Grishaver, Joel L. 2007. "Teaching Jewishly." Torah Aura Productions, October 15, 2007.

congregation and congregants themselves. But afterschool Hebrew school required work that I perceived to be pointless: creativity with lesson plans, scheduling, ordering art supplies—and that seemed to never be good enough to my cohort of wild animals. They probably weren't even *that bad*, but I had such respect for my Jewish upbringing and education that this level of disorganization and lack of real progress all felt like such an utter waste of everyone's time.

Contrast that disaster with Jack's measurable growth. We made large flashcards and worked slowly for Jack to recognize letters. He kept them in the closet/tutoring room, and I begged him to practice more without me. For ease, I enlarged the font size of any prayer we were told to spend time learning. Two to four sentences would take up an entire eight and a half by eleven-inch sheet of paper. We would never move on to more material until we mastered the verse or phrase we were working on, even if it was something small. This approach gave Jack a sense of accomplishment with each session. We would always discuss the meaning of the prayer and I'd ask Jack what he thought about it theologically or literarily. Sometimes, during our 3 p.m. lessons, Jack would have a fifteen-minute check-in or assessment with his Hebrew school educator. I'd almost never have any advance notice of these check-ins. He'd have to get on a FaceTime or Skype call via his iPhone 9—the screen wasn't even three inches wide. The educator would screen share a prayer that he would need to read or chant. Often, Jack had that same prayer amongst our stack of papers. Many times, it was the exact passage that we had been working on, however, on the tiny phone screen he wouldn't recognize a thing. He'd struggle to see the small letters and fail to fluidly read the prayer. I would have to bite my tongue and not prompt him or get frustrated. In front of only me, Jack could chant entire nine verses of a prayer like the Shema/V'ahavta.[49] Once he felt under pressure, all of our hard work went out of the window. It was like watching a car crash in slow motion. I was protective over Jack, both in his sense of confidence and also over how this would reflect on him. I really felt and still feel this process was a terrible way to assess a child.

I spoke to my mother, who has been a school counselor for at-risk youth in the Washington, DC area and was currently serving as a licensed volunteer social worker with the Red Cross. We agreed that Jack had some performance anxiety that was making him seem underprepared in his Jewish studies. What's worse is that this also happened in his school assessments. His performance anxiety was activated with all types of tests. Ironically, Jack confided in me that he would often say this same prayer, Shema/V'ahavta, when he was handing in a test or at times that he was really scared. I never judged Jack and never even asked if he had any sort of diagnosis. What I observed in real time was enough for me to see that we needed to make him feel super comfortable with any material before moving to the new prayers. And we had to work on his confidence. That's how I proceeded. His mother, Tali, always asked how he was doing and I would gush about Jack's intellect, sweetness, and depth of character. I would remind them that he needed to do flashcards and homework and she seemed satisfied with my paragraphs of text messages. She had her hands full with other children, a fine jewelry business, and running her household. She also wanted Jack to mature and take responsibility for practicing and polishing his Hebrew passages. Jack was her oldest, and his anxiousness was on her radar.

Over time, his siblings started to join in our lessons too—

---

49 Deuteronomy: Chapter 6 - Daily prayer: "Hear Oh Israel and You shall love G-d with all your heart, soul and might."

whether when we cooked special foods, like latkes for Hanukkah, or made arts and crafts. Eventually, Jack's parents allowed me to bring my dog to sessions. Tali first felt like their older dog might not tolerate my dog. Soon, the family adopted a Cavapoo named Sunflower, a little dog that was similar in size and breed to Scout. The two of them became a puppy couple and we planned a puppy wedding to learn about the customs of a Jewish wedding. I made it out of the shoe closet, and would sometimes teach Jack in the den, the Hamptons, backyard, living room, the kitchen, or his room.

When the pandemic hit, Jack went to live in his house in Southampton but we continued Zoom lessons without skipping a beat. I watched him grow in front of my screen. We joked, checked in with each other, struggled together with the frustrating technological connections, and I taught him about the historic Black Lives Matter movement and protests in New York City. I told him how I would check on his townhouse on my daily walks around Central Park to occupy my time alone.

At the start of one lesson, Jack confessed ominously: "Becky, I have to tell you something. My parents decided that it was better that they stay best friends but not be a couple anymore. So, they are going to get a divorce. I just think you should know." I was shocked. I'm glad it was on Zoom because I did not expect it and didn't know how to react. Jack wasn't even twelve years old, but as he choked on the hard lump in his throat, I realized how this child was losing so much of his innocence right before my eyes: worldwide illness, racism, unrest in the streets, and now this seismic shift of his own family. It all had to rock his world. He was smart and knew a lot was changing around him. He was becoming a man.

The same summer his older dog, Ranger, passed away. Jack asked if we could design a Jewish funeral service for Ranger. I adapted one of my standard funeral services and edited a PDF to create a memorial service program for a dog. I customized it with Ranger's name and included standard Jewish liturgy. On a Zoom session, we said all the prayers together and Jack felt a lot better. Obviously, plenty of observant Jews would feel that Jewish dog funerals are both sacrilegious and flat out wrong. But Jack was still learning about Jewish customs. Death and mourning are a big part of life. Ranger was like an older brother and a member of the family for his entire life. Before he would have to experience any *human* relative passing away, I saw this as an excellent opportunity to teach Jack about Jewish funerals. I sent the service to his parents but I'm not sure that they ever did the service in totality as a family. The dog funeral was for Jack and me to learn and process in a deeply personal and spiritual way. It was for him to access prayers when he needed them, and learn how to add his voice to words of deep sadness and mourning.

A few days later, I went out to the Hamptons to visit the many kids I work with and conduct some lessons. It was during the COVID-19 pandemic, so there was a lot of anxiety about testing, conducting sessions strictly outdoors, and only with those who tested negative. I was a regular at CityMD for PCR tests in a dual attempt to keep everyone healthy and to keep my sanity. I was one of the only in-person educators in the Hamptons. Most children had finished their school year online. I was definitely the only rabbi willing to drive several hours out east and house hop. If you've never been out to the Hamptons, it's a mix between Beverly Hills and the middle of nowhere. It's like a private beach with a community that centers around golfing, tennis, pools, the beach, and a few small strips of shops and restaurants. The nightlife is either a dive-bar concert venue called the Stephen Talkhouse or cheesy clubs. My clients spend their summer nights house party hopping. The Weisers lived in Southampton. Even though they had just announced their separation, Tali and Michael, Jack's father, lived in houses across the street from each other. This setup made it even easier for the kids to switch from house to house and parent to parent. To this day I have no idea why Tali and Michael had houses so close together. It's not easy to procure two properties practically beachside in the Hamptons. Neither house was brand new. *Was one an investment property? Or was it like they expected this separation one day? Maybe it was like a plan b or hedge?* (After all the dad was in investment banking.) *It could have been a really nice staff house or grandparents house?* I don't know and I try not to think about it too hard.

When I was out there, I actually met Michael for the first time. He was so charming, smart, and warm. I could see why people would trust him with their assets; besides having the best head of curly blonde hair, he had a smile that was bright and honest. He was interested and asked analytical questions. I recognized the curiosity and intellect of his children from our first conversation. Michael was also talking about moving up Jack's bar mitzvah date to be right before his forty-fifth birthday. This idea came up because they were going to send Jack away for a spring semester in London. That meant Jack would have less than five months to learn a Torah portion. He would have his bar mitzvah at the premature age of twelve. It would mean our lessons together would have to transition from working on prayers to gearing up for a typical Reform bar mitzvah during the pandemic—whatever that meant. Synagogues were limiting attendance to groups of thirty people. They were insisting people wear masks. Many Reform congregations forced all services to be performed online and truncated to account for Zoom fatigue. If services were held in person, they only allowed a fraction of congregants into their sanctuaries to limit exposure to the virus. For Jack's bar mitzvah, we would have to learn approximately ten to twelve verses from the Torah with Hebrew characters. Jack would prepare them with notes and color coding but come the actual day, he would have to do it all with none of those crutches or cheat sheets. With so much uncertainty of what the day would look like, plus balancing Jack's performance anxiety and new family structure, this plan seemed like a recipe for failure.

Jack wanted me to be up on the religious stage, or bima, right by his side. It doesn't quite work like that. Even though I was a rabbi, I didn't have privileges at Jack's synagogue to be on the bima with his clergy. Actually, because of the pandemic, the rabbi with whom he had a relationship wasn't even going to be next to him. Only the female cantor, with whom he had a few check-in sessions, was allowed to be up there with him. It's a little bit like being a doctor. Just because you're a medical professional, doesn't mean you have privileges at every hospital. I am not a member of the Reform movement or an employee of Temple Israel, so there was no way they'd let me up there next to Jack.

Cantor Irena Altshul has an other-worldly voice, a beautiful mezzo soprano, and an Eastern European way about her. I have nothing but admiration for her cantorial talents. I admire her bravery and ability to ascend the mountain she's had to climb to become senior cantor at a major market synagogue like Temple Israel. However, I felt an ever-present tension in our communication. We both had busy jobs but she had priorities that were perhaps more complex than simply making Jack comfortable. She had a rigorous schedule of synagogue duties. She had to treat all children equally and not allow for certain standards to be bent or accommodations to be made for Jack's needs. That was antithetical to my modus operandi. I worked first and foremost for the family. I tried to be a team player but nonetheless would not let Jack be a casualty among the many due to failing synagogue systems and a formulaic bar mitzvah program.

When Jack asked if he could have his white binder with all of his notes and materials up by the Torah in case he needed to glance over, both rabbi and cantor said he should not have any sort of a crutch or help. Rabbi David especially said that this was the one time in his life that he should try to read from the Torah without help. I totally disagreed. I told the cantor offline about Jack's increased anxiety as the date approached—but it didn't change her mind. The Torah has none of the pronunciation notations and singing notes that a child usually learns with. Many children simply memorize their portions. If you watch Netflix's *You Are So Not Invited to My Bat Mitzvah*, the main character, Stacy Friedman, just memorizes her Torah portion with phone recordings. I strongly recommend against this and instead encourage a child to focus on their reading skills. If a child reads and tries to use the Hebrew text, even if the Torah uses an ornate and complicated font, they have a better chance of not getting totally lost. For Jack, a bar mitzvah, during the pandemic and his parent's divorce, was a moment in his life unlike any other. If he had to glance at his notes, we as compassionate educators and mindful professionals should help him and not shame him for needing accommodation. Singing prayers and all of his learning was still tremendous, especially given his specific anxieties and all the year's challenges. I wasn't babying him—I was scared for him. The clergy's disapproval of using any colored sheets or notes with Hebrew vowels or transliteration over one or two words *did* motivate Jack more than ever to practice. But it was inevitable that he was going to stumble in front of his community. I'm not convinced that doing things one hundred percent authentically and stumbling was better than performing smoothly but with a crutch. Either would have been a noteworthy accomplishment. I felt as though the temple was failing to see the boy in front of them. These were unprecedented times of online learning, contact tracing, and viruses with undocumented effects on children's abilities to focus. *How could the shul be so inflexible?* It's not as if they are an Orthodox congregation that made no allowances or reforms; they had a female cantor; they made plans to break the Sabbath with a big screen monitor to broadcast the service. Nothing made sense to me. I felt totally powerless to help Jack other than to just rehearse and rehearse. The weeks and days leading up to Jack's bar mitzvah felt increasingly like I lived at Tali's apartment.

When the day of Jack's bar mitzvah came, I was so emotional. There were only twenty-five or so people allowed in the sanctuary and I was pretty surprised that the clergy was still so petrified of COVID-19 that they wouldn't enter the sanctuary while the family took pictures on the bima. I had spent every waking second with the family. Whatever COVID status they had, I had. I hugged everyone a hundred times. I held onto Jack's materials at my seat and beamed with pride as he posed with his three younger siblings. I sat on the side of the sanctuary with Michael, both because I had a better view of Jack and also because more of Tali's side was present in the sanctuary. The rabbi entered from a back entrance, masked, and stayed behind a wall of plexiglass through the entire ceremony. A large sixty-five-foot television geared up with Zoom provided the approved private guests a live stream of the one-hour service.

Jack seemed nervous but as prepared as he was going to be. He did an excellent job. He performed all of his prayers as expected and without noticeably stumbling. He looked happy and handsome. When it came time for his Torah portion, the cantor seemed like she wanted to just set the Torah down and let him read from it, but he needed more help than that. She had to point and give him the first word for his three sections of Torah. Defiantly, I snuck his colored notes in the outside sleeve of his white binder so he could have them near him as a security blanket. They were marked up with drawings to help trigger his memory for words, highlighting similar sounds and tunes. I don't actually think he glanced at them, but knowing they were there was helpful to him.

At most, Jack probably made two or three mistakes. I was in the front row on the edge of my seat, singing along and crying for his achievement. I was overjoyed that he got through it and could celebrate. The final moment of the bar mitzvah service was a surprise that was Rabbi David's deep genius. There's an old rabbinic adage that on Yom Kippur, a boy who couldn't master the words of Hebrew prayers just let out a crow of a rooster; this was to make a raw sound to reach the heavens and G-d. Jack may not have been great at Hebrew but he had a way to do something similar. A few years prior, Jack had discovered a large ram's horn in his storage room. As a ten-year-old, he picked it up and just started to blow and realized he was not only able, but really good at blowing the ritual ram's horn. This horn, or *shofar*, was typically used to announce the new Jewish year and surrounding holidays. Jack was among many children invited to blow the shofar at his synagogue High Holiday services. Rabbi David's idea now was that Jack should blow the shofar at the end of *his* service. I brought Jack's shofar and hid it by my feet. At the end of his ceremony, Rabbi David gave the cue and I brought it to Jack on the stage. He let a big celebratory blast rip through his congregation. It was an epic way to usher in his adulthood.

With virtually no discussion, I also started to teach Jack's brother, Julien, via Zoom. Julien was a totally different kid. He was the middle child of four siblings. He rode off the radar, was as cool as a cucumber, and was seemingly unattached. He was smart and funny. If you squinted and listened closely, Julien was probably mocking you. Julien's best friends were his brother Jack and his cousin Zev. As is the case with many Syrian boys, Julien's mother, Tali, was his everything. Michael would become his role model. At eleven years old, Julien was a shrewd businessman.

Like many city kids, he was trading and selling designer sneakers for a profit. Julien idolized Kanye West for his rap music and for creating Yeezys. Julien wore Yeezy slides or sneakers to every session. Anytime he struggled to pronounce Hebrew words that included the sound "yay," I would paste a clip art photo of Kanye West's face above the word to make him laugh and help him sound out the syllable.

Julien's bar mitzvah ceremony was scheduled a full year after Jack's and our process was totally different. I had already been teaching him letters weekly via Zoom, so by January of 2021, Julien could recognize most of them. By the fall of 2022, he could smoothly read and chant basic prayers. I no longer reported to the Hebrew school educator about Julien or any of the kids. I taught Julien prayers in the same order I had taught his older brother, and we had way more time to talk about politics, Jewish history, Torah stories, and holidays. Because we started his prayers and workload much sooner, by the time Julien went to camp in June, he already knew his entire Torah portion.

As the 2022 school year started, public sentiment towards Israel and antisemitism really interested Julien. The world was going bananas. The pandemic was easing but economic and social implications of the virus were becoming more evident. Additionally, race, racism, gender, and sexuality were constant topics even in middle school. Contrast that with his upper-class bubble. The lifestyles of the Upper East Side had returned like the roaring twenties. Dinner parties, shopping, and weekend trips all resumed. Masks were only a thing for people who were overly anxious or sick themselves. Fortune favored the brave. Kids had become even more dependent on their wireless devices. With social distance even from one's own parents and grandparents, children were used to less supervision. Kids like Julien, who were independent learners, thrived during COVID-19 times.

They could make as much of their lessons as they desired. They figured out ways to fake their Zoom attendance during online school. They'd also trick their parents into thinking they were using their computer for studies, when really, they were gaming or looking up other things. Parents were so happy their kids seemed to be independent; I observed parents fitting in more and more personal appointments while they had otherwise spent time with their children. To make up for the lost time, kids and parents were moving at warp speed, but often on different planes of existence.

The Weiser kids were really excited for that summer. I came out a few times to visit them in the Hamptons. I also conducted virtual lessons with Julien all summer while he was at sleepaway camp. Meanwhile, I was getting closer to making a deal selling a reality-documentary series about my work as an on-call rabbi looking for love in the big city. Reese Witherspoon's company Hello Sunshine had optioned my life story and after a few months of negotiations, filmed what the industry calls a "sizzle reel" or "trailer." The trailer was to be used to sell the show to networks. I could write a whole additional chapter in this book about why that show never sold. But Witherspoon's company understood how unique and interesting both my work and clients could be for audiences worldwide. Unfortunately, the way the show was packaged could be seen as yet another white woman looking for love in the New York City—been there, done that. Additionally, the strategy of the production company and producers was strange: they didn't want me, the main character of the series, to be in any of the pitch rooms. Once they wanted me in the pitch rooms, Hello Sunshine's whole strategy pivoted and the climate towards Jews in Hollywood became increasingly cloudy. Unfortunately, the show couldn't make it off the development shelf, where it remains. The Weisers, though, loved asking about updates and really wanted to be in the show if ever it made it off the ground.

Right at the start of the new school year, "THE JEWS" catapulted into the popular culture everyday news because of Kanye West. In case you don't remember the timeline and how it all started, I'll lay it out as the *New York Times* does.[50]

- September 15, 2022: Ye announced he would be ending his relationship with Gap and opening his own stores.

- October 3, 2022: During Paris Fashion Week, Ye presented his new line YZY. He and Candace Owens, a provocative Fox News commentator, wore matching oversized T-shirts with a printed slogan "White Lives Matter." Bloggers, fashion editors, and even the Anti-Defamation League responded calling the shirt and its slogan hate speech, as the slogan originated with White supremacists.

- Ye explained that his use of the slogan was a response to perceived corruption and failures of the Black Lives Matter movement. He also engaged in a social media bullying campaign against *Vogue* editor Gabriella Karefa-Johnson for her outspoken disapproval of the shirt.[51]

- October 7, 2022: Ye's long-time friend Sean Combs, aka "Diddy," reached out to try and get Ye to realize the

50 Tumin, Remy. 2022. "Kanye West Faces Costly Fallout: A Timeline." The *New York Times*, December 19, 2022. https://www.nytimes.com/article/kanye-west-timeline.html.

51 Friedman, Vanessa. 2022. "There Is No Excuse for Ye's 'White Lives Matter' Shirt." The *New York Times*, October 4, 2022. https://www.nytimes.com/2022/10/04/style/yeezy-kanye-west-paris-fashion-week.html.

multiple errors of his ways. Ye texted Diddy that he was being controlled by Jewish people and posted a screenshot of their conversation on Instagram. After the screenshot was liked by tens of thousands of Ye's followers, it was flagged and Ye was restricted from Instagram.

- October 8, 2022: Ye lashed out against Jewish people in a series of tweets. Ye tweeted: "I'm a bit sleepy tonight but when I wake up I'm going death con 3 On JEWISH PEOPLE. The funny thing is I actually can't be Anti Semitic because black people are actually Jew also You guys have toyed with me and tried to black ball anyone whoever opposes your agenda." The tweet was seen, shared, and hearted by thousands before it was removed by Twitter and he was locked out of the platform.[52]

- October 15, 2022: Ye made other public appearances via podcasts, continuing to spew antisemitism and even denied George Floyd's murder—claiming it was an overdose of fentanyl. He blamed a "Jewish media mafia," and took no responsibility.

- October 21, 2022: Companies finally started severing ties with Ye. Balenciaga and one of his agencies, Creative Arts Agencies, ended relationships.

- October 25, 2022: Due to enormous pressure, Adidas dropped the design and sneaker partnership with Ye,

---

52 Cramer, Philissa, and Ron Kampeas. 2022. "A Clear Violence: Understanding Kanye's Tweet Vowing 'Death Con 3' on Jews." The Times of Israel, October 12, 2022. https://www.timesofisrael.com/a-clear-violence-understanding-kanyes-tweet-vowing-death-con-3-on-jews/.

costing them 250 million dollars just in one year. *Forbes* reported that Ye's net worth was cut by more than 1.5 billion dollars and he consequently lost his billionaire status.

- There were more television interviews, responses, and public commentaries. Notably there was the November 13, 2022 monologue on *Saturday Night Live* delivered by Dave Chapelle (over which even my husband and I cannot agree. I found it offensive and harmful to Jewish people, not funny, and a calculated dog whistle to stir more anti-Jewish feelings).

- December 1, 2022: Ye appeared in an Alex Jones episode with a ski mask, prop bible, fly net, and bottle of Yoo-hoo to represent Benjamin Netanyahu. Multiple times on the episode, he praised Hitler, the mass murdering nazi who was one of the all-time most evil people to ever exist.[53] "Every human being has value that they brought to the table, especially Hitler," he told Jones. He also denied the Holocaust.[54]

You might wonder how I handled this as a teacher and rabbi who is interested in pop culture, fashion, and social media. At the first whiff of the controversy in early October, my students and I were

---

53 Reynolds, Nick. 2022. "Alex Jones, Kanye West Argue Over Nazis, Hitler." *Newsweek*, December 1, 2022. https://www.newsweek.com/alex-jones-kanye-west-argue-over-nazis-hitler-1763997.

54 Aniftos, Rania. 2022. "Kanye West Praises Hitler in Alex Jones Interview: 'I Also Love Nazis.'" *Billboard*, December 1, 2022. https://www.billboard.com/music/music-news/kanye-west-praises-adolf-hitler-1235179653/.

tracking the developments. It became a five- to ten-minute part of every lesson, to unpack the latest *mishigas,* craziness, that Ye did or said. Ye drama often interested my male students more than my female students, who were typically die-hard Taylor Swift fans, aka "Swifties." If you don't know, there is actually a long-standing rivalry between Swift and Ye ever since he interrupted her acceptance speech at the 2009 MTV Video Music Awards and shamed her for winning over Beyoncé. Swifties, which most of my ten- to thirteen-year-old students are, couldn't care less about Ye. But young Jewish men have a thing for urban culture and hip hop. And I'll admit, Ye is an incredible rapper and artist. Plus, kids love fancy sneakers. Nearly all of my male students had at least one pair of Yeezy sneakers or slides. This was more than just Twitter drama, this was *relevant.* I was texting them articles, and they were writing back. What's crazy is their schools avoided the topic almost entirely. Coming off a year of BLM, there was no procedure nor vocabulary to navigate a minefield like West's public demise that intersected with race, religion, and mental illness.

No young man felt more of a dilemma than Julien. Remember, we often did lessons inside of a shoe closet! Since his parents had split up, the large mansion on Fifth Avenue had become his father's house, and our tutoring room was solely a home for his father's shoes. He had several pairs of Yeezys and several pairs of Balenciaga shoes. Scout would often like to rest by crawling over the shelf with the handsome leather dress shoes and burying his fluffy face in one of the identical brown lace up Pradas. Julien and I followed the weekly West drama and would dissect each insult and occurrence. He'd always come back to just how mind-blowing it all was. He'd ask again and again why Ye would choose to lash out at the Jews. We talked about the history of Louis Farrakhan. We compared and contrasted his antisemitic remarks with Kyrie Irving's and weighed the public reaction. I told him I would no longer allow him to wear the Yeezy slides to our lessons. His consumerism was an expression of his values. It was my right to not allow a mentally unstable Jew-hater into our shoe-closet classroom. Several times in that October and November, Julien had friends over during our lessons. They asked me if it was true that they couldn't have Kanye's music at their bar mitzvah parties. I replied, "If you ask me, the answer is no. There is enough good music to fill a party." They'd often protest that he was the greatest rapper and I'd say I didn't care. I'd remind them the rapper literally praised Hitler, the man who sought to wipe us off the planet. West hated them and their families and was saying inflammatory things that would result in real vandalism and violence against all of our people. Enough with the glorification of him as white-passing fanboys. West's music was not welcome.

I knew there might be a way to tie this moment into Julien's mitzvah project for a deeper connection to fighting against anti-semitism, pride in his people, and a chance to make a sizable donation to a charity that would do something to protect Jewish people. To paraphrase a saying I would often hear at Chabad houses, "if you want to know what's happening in the current events, look in the Torah." Julien's Torah portion was the iconic scene of Jacob's Ladder. The portion is called "Vayeitzei." The scene starts with Jacob running away from his home in Canaan/Israel because he has just stolen a blessing from his older brother Esau. While on his journey in the desert, Jacob makes a pillow out of a stone and falls asleep. He dreams of angels ascending and descending a ladder. Then G-d promises Jacob that the land on which he lies is his inheritance. However, since Jacob is full of anxiety, he wants to make a deal with G-d. Jacob negotiates that *only if* G-d provides him with food, safety, and lets him one day return to this place, then he will accept G-d. When he wakes up, Jacob erects a stone pillar at this place and names it Beth El. Interestingly, the synagogue I grew up in was named Beth El, and above their bima, hung silk tapestries of the angels going up and down ladders.

The beautiful symbolism of this portion often leads people to focus on the dream with the ladder. One of my previous students working with Rabbi David had the same portion and I remembered that Rabbi David gave him supplementary rabbinic commentary to read about the dream and angels. Julien got a similar packet and I could tell I should work within Rabbi David's direction but still dealing with the uniqueness of Julien's interests. It was decidedly evident from those modern commentary packets that the angels going both up and down the ladder were the good people on earth—like nurses, doctors, and teachers.

Still, this was not enough for Julien to analyze. He saw that Jacob was under personal threat and experiencing fear. He was not sure if G-d was going to protect him on his journey. His surroundings were changing and there were many unknowns. Julien understood the moment of fear in Jacob as parallel to the moment of rising fear in the American Jewish Community. As a man with four times as many social media followers as there were Jews in the world, Ye inflamed hatred. By spreading anti-Jewish messages, he was contributing to potential and resulting acts of violence against Jewish people and vandalism against property. Julien was looking for more angels on earth to help with a rising problem that was really threatening him and his community. Much like Jacob, he wanted to make a deal with G-d. With his bar mitzvah, he wanted to vow his lasting commitment to the Jewish People, but couldn't do it if he didn't feel safe.

It happens to be that my best friend Noa is married to a retired Lieutenant Commander of the Israeli Navy Seals, Shayetet 13. Through Oran, I became involved in the National Leadership Council of American Friends of Israeli Navy SEALs (AFINS). In

Israel, nearly everyone serves in the army for at least two years. You don't have to fight: you can be a lookout, a translator in an intelligence unit, a musician in the army orchestra, or just get people coffee all day. But the best of the best want to fight for their country. They want to protect their families from enemies that constantly threaten Israel's civilian population. There are many elite units, but none as selective as the Israeli Navy Shayetet 13. The unit specializes in sea-to-land incursions, counterterrorism, hostage rescue, and much more in the sea, air, and on land. Often those who spend time in the unit wind up spending three to nine years in the unit because it takes so much training. However, because of their longer term of service, they start the rest of their lives a little later. This impacts their families financially. And G-d forbid someone ends their service injured or even dies while serving, this impacts them and their families as well. It's ironic that we sacrifice our best and are forced to lose them in order to survive as a people. I told Julien through the years of teaching about the many brave operations that the Sha-yetet would pull off. He found those stories really interesting. He also loved the water and was great at surfing and sailing. It seemed like a natural fit that he'd have an interest in the Israeli navy and how they act like angels to protect the Jewish people.

I decided to invite Julien to an AFINS gala, near his house on the Upper East Side. I really wanted Julien to meet a few of the former and active soldiers. Some of them were just what you'd imagine: tall, buff, tan, and some even came in a modified uniform. Many of them looked of average build, and explained in small groups that it wasn't about how tall or strong you were, but how you performed, improved, and how you grew through the training. I wanted Julien to be proud to be a Jew. I wanted him to meet examples of strong Jewish men, besides his family and the other successful men of the Upper East Side. These men were real-life heroes. His father came along and I was so happy that Michael wanted to stay through the presentation. We heard a member of the unit discuss a mission, its challenges, and how it was completed. We learned how hard it was on all of those who participated. The retired SEAL was charming and looked like he could run a company and save your life. His story was inspiring and made all the American Jews in the room feel incredibly indebted. These were the real people keeping us safe on the front lines.

There was then a moment when the master of ceremonies for the evening started asking for donations and pledges. The highest pledge was to sponsor an Israeli SEAL for three years of college in Israel. Julien's family immediately raised their hands. In honor of Julien's bar mitzvah, Michael and Julien felt inspired to give that gift. Julien felt really great about being a big donor for the night. I felt great about bringing Julien to meet these brave men. One of the former captains, now in his fifties, told Julien he was so inspired that a young twelve-year-old boy was taking such interest in the Israeli Navy SEALs that he was going to send him a book that helped him decide he wanted to be a member of the Shayetet 13. Another SEAL, who was finished with his service and worked for an American Jewish non-profit, offered to come to Julien's service. He gave Julien a necklace that he wore during his entire service. He was so touched that Julien wanted to give of his time and effort to support his unit, it was the least he could do. That former SEAL also spent time with Julien's youngest brother, Dipper, teaching him introductory *krav maga,* Israeli martial arts. That same man returned to Israel immediately after the October 7th Hamas attack to serve in the reserves. AFINS recently sent a letter from the very student that just completed their first year of college due to Julien's scholarship. Without Julien acting like a financial angel, these real-life angels could not support the Jewish people, Israel, and her allies in the way that they do.

Julien's bar mitzvah ceremony was less teary than others. His grandmother, who I've become close with, describes him like a cat—as soon as you get close to him, he scampers off and acts aloof. He worked hard, needed me for lessons and help, but wasn't emotionally attached; maybe this was because we both knew he'd do a great job and I didn't have to protect him through the process. He's also really funny and sharp. At his service, he was independent and poised. He chanted beautifully and strongly. Even if he made one or two blunders, he'd shake his head, smile, and make it through. That kind of confidence ensures his success in just about everything. The best moment of his service was his d'var Torah, or speech. It is rewritten here.

Hello everyone and Shabbat Shalom. As I celebrate becoming a bar mitzvah, I am grateful that all of my friends and family are here to be a part of my big day. I go to a great middle school— my parents chose it because it is academically rigorous and the student body is diverse. However, that means I'm one of the only Jews in my class. As St. Bernard's is a Catholic School, we have prayer groups every week that often seem foreign to me. Today, it is really nice to share my religion with my community of friends and family and have a chance to stand on the bima, as an adult, chanting in Hebrew.

Now, let's talk about my Torah Portion: Vayeitzei. I'm sure we've all been there—You've had a big fight with your brother and he tells you he's going to kill you! Well, that's what has just happened to Jacob. Now on the run, his adrenalin taps out and he takes a rest. Jacob dreams about a ladder from here to heaven with angels. Some angels are going up the ladder to heaven and some are coming down to earth. Then, he gets a special message from G-d. G-d blesses Jacob with the entire land for him and his future descendants. By the way, this land is the future State of Israel. Then Jacob makes a special marker out of the stone that was his pillow, naming it "Beyt El," or "House of G-d." He continued to come up with terms for his continued belief in G-d: G-d must provide protection on his journey, both from enemies and the elements, and provide him a safe return back home—then and only then will Jacob accept G-d.

The part of the Torah portion that interested me the most was that there were angels going up and down the ladder. I studied many rabbinical commentaries that urged me to think about the angels going up the ladder as good people on earth. I read an article, "Understanding Jacob's Ladder" by Pinchas Lieser, who is a psychologist and commentator with Jerusalem Elul Institute. He wrote:

> *We can think of "ascent" as an opportunity for spiritual growth and service and of "descent" as re-entering the external world trying to change it for good. In the words of the great Hasidic Master, Rabbi Menachem Mendel Morgensztern of Kotzk, interpreting a verse of Psalms, "The heavens are the heavens of G-d, and the earth is given to human beings—that is, to make of the earth a heaven."*

There are angels here on earth who try to make the world more like heaven, or a more perfect place. They are the heroes who constantly do work to help those in need. They are doctors, soldiers, teachers, and even parents—sometimes. But sometimes it is hard to trust in those providers and systems. Jacob didn't just let the vision of the angels suffice and quell his anxiety. Like a typical, anxious, Jewish guy, he needed extra reassurance from G-d that he was going to be okay. Now that I'm such an expert in Hebrew, I noticed that the same Hebrew word with the root letters of *shin, mem,* and *reysh,* spelling out *shamar,* or *protect,* comes up again and again in the text. Jacob is obsessed with feeling protected on his journey. He wants to make sure that those angels around him will protect him, as he is really scared.

I think I have a unique reading of this passage because I see echoes of myself in Jacob. Okay, okay, my brothers Jack, Maier, and Dipper have never threatened to kill me, but I am growing increasingly concerned about the safety of our people—the Jewish people. Jacob is nervous that his life and future are in danger and it is sometimes our reality here in New York that we are. Antisemitism is always on my mind. Year after year, the Anti-Defamation League and FBI have reported increases of crimes directed at Jews. This really hit me this fall, both as I was preparing for this day and since TikTok became obsessed with discussing Kanye West's various meltdowns and rants towards the Jews. My peers and I used to think Kanye West was one of the greatest artists of all time and the most talented fashion designer. But now, because of his far-reaching antisemitic statements, I feel a difference in the country's attitude against Jewish people— I notice hateful graffiti, I hear more disturbing jokes from other comedians, and my parents have talked about whether or not I can wear a Jewish Star necklace—especially because I take the subway. I feel outnumbered when I go past a hateful crowd of people saying hurtful things outside the Barclay's Center. Kyrie Irving tweeted about an obscure movie and the whole NBA was angry at the Jews. I no longer feel comfortable wearing my favorite shoes, Yeezys, and I have banned Ye's music at my party tonight. While studying for my bar mitzvah, there were FBI warnings about increased threats on Jewish institutions and I've been both worried and interested in what I can do to help my people. At any given moment, I was unsure if I'd have any sneakers to wear. I would ask over and over why so much hate was directed *at the Jews. While I am proud to be Jewish, I often worry about our collective future.*

Through writing this d'var Torah, I thought that I could be like one of the angels going down the ladder, trying to re-enter the world to leave it better than it was before. I have learned that a big part of feeling safe is feeling protected. While I know I always have G-d, the other thing that makes me feel the most safe to be a Jew is the strength of the Israeli Defense Forces. My mitzvah project was to support heroes and angels of our fellow Jewish People. I learned about an elite unit of the Israeli Navy, The Shayetet 13, or Israeli Navy SEALs. My dad and I attended a night of tribute where we met many active and alumni men from the unit. I learned about some of their amazing and dangerous missions. I was riveted by the risks they take to help people in Israel and all over the region. There is an American charity, American Friends of Israeli Navy SEALs, that raises funds for college scholarships, post-traumatic stress disorder therapy programs, and financial aid to those who are injured. For my Mitzvah Project, I am sponsoring the college education of one of the soldiers when they are done with their service. I also hope to host a lecture event with my friends and peer group with the unit so they can learn more about the values of these brave men. They put everything on the line for their people and country. They give me inspiration and pride in who I am and could one day become. In turn, I can be like an angel for them, supporting them with my voice and donations. They really inspire me.

Becoming a man, or a bar mitzvah, is about understanding our place in this world. As I ascend the ladder of adulthood, I know I will encounter many times when I pray for G-d's help and strength. But I also believe in our ability, as a strong Jewish community, to help each other and step up with strength for each other. In every generation they rise up against us. But in every generation, we have to protect ourselves. We have to be our own angels, watching over the health and happiness of our people. Let's not let anything get in the way of our dreams. Shabbat Shalom.

I still continue to teach the two youngest children in the family every Sunday afternoon. I alternate between the mother and father's homes which are just a few blocks apart. I feel like a member of their modern family. I tell their youngest boys, Maier and Dipper, that I will cry my face off when they become b'nai mitzvah. Dipper is dyslexic so I've been working with him in creative ways since he was seven years old. Maier reads beautifully and has learned many songs and prayers even in just fifth grade. Our weekly lessons are joyous, about holidays, Torah stories, current events, and slowly build on cumulative learning. The children each have several copies of workbooks and papers of prayers at both houses, yet we always seem to print out new materials at the start of every lesson. I mark up their pages and then take photos of our notes and we build upon our work using a library in my iPhoto cloud. Often, we bake challah, do arts and crafts, and cook specialty holiday foods with Tali. During the Israel-Hamas war, when Jews were decidedly taking down *mezuzot* from their doorposts, Michael asked me if we could dedicate some of our two-hour family lesson time to putting a new stone mezuzah up outside the house. During the first hour of the lesson, I had taught Maier the blessing we recite while affixing a mezuzah and we went over a melody for the *Shehecheyanu* blessing, a prayer for doing things for the first time. Huddled in the chilly fall weather, with our dogs, the boys recited the blessings as the father, their hero, hung a mezuzah and all of us affirmed with "Amen."

Michael mentioned he didn't know where the mezuzah came from. Julien chimed in quickly, "Dad, that was one of my bar mitzvah gifts."

"Perfect! Now your bar mitzvah is protecting our house."

The message from the Weiser case: the world and families will continue to change; if we want religion to be important in people's lives, then we have to see and acknowledge the lives people live. Children have specific needs and they often do not fit the one-size-fits-all Hebrew school model. Advocate for your children. Advocate for your students. Find real metrics for progress. Not everyone can afford to have a supplementary teacher, but you can try to change the synagogue from within if you feel the system is broken. Or start your own school. Have a teacher who finds a way to interest your children and eases their anxieties. Have a provider who cares about the spiritual well-being of your family. Be bold to teach the next generation about the enemies that surround our people and threaten our well-being. Give them tools and talking points to join the conversation or fight. Do whatever you can to strengthen the agencies that protect us. They provide security and assurance that Jews will persevere through anything. We are capable of standing on a religious stage to represent adulthood and our families, just as Jews are capable of protecting ourselves and defending our right to exist. These lessons are so important when instructing strong confident adults.

CONFESSION VI:
Not all Jews believe in G-d, and despite what you think, that's ok.

"Your word is a lamp to my feet, a light for my path."
—PSALM 119: 105

Case Study 3

I met Lea and Archer before I met their parents. As it goes with Jewish children in New York City, some families prefer to leave institutional Hebrew school because they find the synagogue options limiting. Such was the problem with Eden's family— typical, liberal, and residing on the Upper West Side. Eden's mom was Jewish and her father was a Jewish convert. Seeking the right fit for their daughter to start learning about traditions when she was nine years old, they called me to organize a small private group. Eden's good friend, Archer, and Archer's big sister Lea, became our three-person, once-a-week, alternative Hebrew class. All three kids studied at Ethical Culture Fieldston School. The school and movement were founded by Felix Adler. As a former Jew, Adler started his own failed social religion called The Ethical Culture Society to experiment with what it would be like to eliminate all the dogma and practice of religion but maintain a set of universal values for society. Founded in 1876, the society's website reads: "Ethical Culture is a Humanist religion to some, and philosophy to others, centered on ethics, not theology, whose mission is to encourage respect for humanity and nature and to create a better world. Members are committed to personal ethical development in their relationships with others and in activities pursuing social justice, environmental stewardship, and engaging in democratic citizenship."[55] While Adler's religion never spread further than this Upper West Side community, what really had sticking power was a prestigious private school, Ethical Culture Fieldston. Fieldston is a part of the Ivy Preparatory School League, made up of other nearby schools including Riverdale Country and Horace Mann—for which I also feel like the resident rabbi. Each year, I serve only a few families who go to Fieldston, as they are notably more liberal in their religious observance.

Our little group met for a year in a grand dining room in Eden's Upper West Side penthouse apartment. One of the walls was entirely made of windows and led out to their apartment's wrap-around terrace. Another wall, behind which I would usually sit, was a customized urban graffiti mural displaying quotes and sayings that were inspirational to the family's daughters. There was gorgeous designer furniture on both sides of their large dining table. Sometimes my dog, Scout, would run around wild with Eden's dog. Occasionally, Archer and Lea would bring their dog, Louis, who was a large, black long-haired retriever. All the dogs would play while we studied bible stories and traditions and did crafts. I worried that my newly-trained puppy would make a mess of the apartment—though he never did. I never went past the threshold of the main house into the bedrooms at Eden's home, and neither did Scout.

I never spoke to Lea and Archer's parents about the content of our lessons. I would just send a divided invoice for our time

---

55   The New York Society for Ethical Culture. n.d. "What Is Ethical Culture?" The New York Society for Ethical Culture. Accessed January 22, 2024. https://ethical.nyc/about/.

together. After a year, Lea and Archer decided not to continue lessons with Eden. I'm pretty sure that Eden decided to work with a different teacher. There was no real end. No big drama, at least that I can remember. Honestly, unless there was a move or divorce, it was pretty rare to have a client discontinue my services. However, twice I had families end my services because my dog had a fight with their puppy. Each of those times, I was mortified and never saw those students again. With Eden's last lesson in the spring of 2017, I expected to never see Archer and Lea again.

To my surprise, I got a call one day in the summer of 2018 from Elizabeth, Lea and Archer's mother. Into the call Elizabeth merged David, her husband, with whom I had never interacted. To my surprise they wanted to continue lessons with the goal of a joint b'nai mitzvah in the summer of 2020. But their vision was one different from any other family I had yet to serve. I'm not sure of the exact words exchanged, but the end result was this: David was a proud Jew, intellectual, lover of Israel, but decidedly not religious. He was an atheist. His wife, Dr. Elizabeth Goldberg, who seemed to be known to everyone as one of the go-to dermatologists in New York City, was less decided about G-d, but non-religious by default. David and Elizabeth wanted our religion, prayer by prayer, presented thoughtfully to their children, discussed, analyzed, and offered almost like a dish for their choosing. The children and I would decide after each prayer, whether or not it should be included in their b'nai mitzvah service. Then, in real time, I would have to figure out what would be permissible or kosher with me. While Reform Judaism literally reformed the rules, requirements, and contents of religious prayer, I was not and still am not a Reform rabbi. With a traditional background, for me, there are certain parts to a Jewish prayer service that must be included. On what was I willing to bend? David was adamant that even though the kids had enough time to learn Hebrew characters and to become literate Hebrew readers, it was not important to them as a family. He wanted content and meaning over sounding out foreign characters. This was really hard for me to cave in on, as I believed that the Hebrew language unifies all Jews globally. However, David had a point: with the thirty lessons a year we would have, the time we would spend learning Hebrew would take away from the deep theological and "Jewy" debates that he wanted his children to engage in and grow from.

On the one hand, I felt like it was antithetical to hold a religious service for nonbelievers. On the other hand, I loved how David and Elizabeth so thoughtfully approached their children's education. They wanted this to actually mean something to them. David was present for almost every lesson. About fifteen feet away in their large open floor plan, on the couch, with Louis the dog, David often chimed in when we discussed current events or analyzed prayers. Many of my students' parents were totally fine with just an invoice at the end of a month. But David and Elizabeth cared deeply about their children's development and learning. They wanted to make sure they were able to grow as individual thinkers. They wanted to make sure that if Archer thought differently from Lea, or differently from mom and dad, that was okay and encouraged. They wanted it all to be fun, and low key and high key. I had a big task on my shoulders. Also, we had a real goal in mind—a b'nai mitzvah to accomplish. We were going to have to learn their Torah portion, a task that includes mastering chanting words in Hebrew along with crafting a thoughtful speech. Lea and Archer cared way more about character analysis of Moses, Joshua, and Caleb and had fun relating their story to modern day historical events. We analyzed the US presidential election, the BLM movement, the COVID-19 pandemic, and multiple operations in the Middle East, then related them all to their Torah portion, the fourth story in the Book of Numbers,

Sh'lach. The plot: Moses sent representative spies from each tribe of Israel to check out Canaan in advance of the nation's arrival and the drama that ensued.

Years later, when I asked David to participate in this chapter, he said verbatim: "I'm sure I'm also influenced by the rising (cresting?) tide of the atheist intelligentsia (Hitchens, Dawkins, Harris) who seemingly struck a raw nerve in 'the West' regarding the corrupted nature of organized religion. In part, my desire as a parent was to allow my kids to decide for themselves how to think about and incorporate religion into their lives. That's what you and I talked about on our first call. And . . . not blowing smoke . . . you really got my kids to think about what it means to be a Jew today and what it means for them individually. Archer definitely feels a stronger connection and will likely continue to explore. Lea? If it helps her get a ten percent discount off some name-brand jeans, she's down. Otherwise . . ."

When I reach back in my memory to recall sessions we had, I remember Archer having more opinions about whether or not he wanted to include or exclude a certain prayer from the service we were planning. My struggle as a young rabbi was to find a balance of validating the feelings and questions of a young man but also safeguarding our age-old tradition. I found my comfort and middle ground in rabbinic precedent. I have collaborated with tens of rabbis throughout my career, whether as an educator, lay cantor, or congregant. Jewish people often say things like "well, at my synagogue we do the prayers like *this*," or "that's not the way *my temple* does it." Within Orthodox Judaism there is a clear structure and expectation to prayer service order. The prayer book is literally called a *siddur,* which mean's ordered program. But once you take a step away from the strictest form of our religion, you are left with a can of worms for wiggle room. I had worked with a freelancing rabbi based out of Los Angeles who edited the many morning blessings. The *Birkot HaShachar*, dawn blessings, are fifteen blessings to be said among the first prayers of the service. Many of the Reform temples do not even say most of the *Shacharit*, morning prayers, or *Pesukei d'Zimra*, psalms of praise sections. There has been a lot of liberal editing and truncation that is unique to each community. A mainstay is the *Amidah*, which is also called the standing prayer: it is a long section of the prayer service that is known to have replaced ancient temple animal sacrifice. Some synagogues only do the first three paragraphs out loud and give a small moment for silent reflection since most of the congregants do not actually pray the silent portion of the prayer in Hebrew. The Torah service and its accompanying blessings that lend to the pomp and circumstance of reading the Torah scroll are also standard across denominations. But the morning warm up prayers became the optional ones for Lea and Archer to cherry pick. I had seen so many other synagogues focus on only one or two of the morning psalms or blessings. Additionally, there was one more logistical reason I decided to put morning blessings on a potential chopping block. The family was planning on holding a b'nai mitzvah service in Israel after a morning hike in the Golan Heights. I was actually unsure if the service was going to be in the morning or in the afternoon. Depending on what time of day a service takes place, certain prayers are not included or swapped out. For example, it makes sense that we thank G-d for waking up only in the morning time; we bless G-d for bringing on the evening only when it actually is evening. While I would have preferred to teach Lea and Archer every single prayer for every type of service, we learned slowly and only met once a week; therefore, the Shacharit prayer structure was open to our editing pen.

All blessings have the same first six words in Hebrew that translate to: "Praised are You, Adonai our G-d, Ruler of the Universe."

We discussed what we learned about our relationship with G-d and as people if this is the way we always worship. Obviously, we have a formal relationship with G-d, as subject and master, and that's the way G-d wants it to stay—or at least the way the rabbis teach. The children generally accepted the idea that G-d has no form and that G-d is referred to as male mostly because Hebrew has no gender-neutral words. Below is a translation of the list of the fifteen blessings standard for morning worship, minus the formulaic introductory words.

1. Who gives our hearts understanding to distinguish day from night.
2. Who has created me in his Image.
3. Who has created me as a descendant of Israel.
4. Who has created me as not as a woman.
5. Who opens the eyes of the blind.
6. Who provides clothing for the naked.
7. Who frees the captive.
8. Who raises up the fallen.
9. Who spread out the earth above the waters.
10. Who has supplied my every want.
11. Who strengthens our steps.
12. Who girds Israel with strength.
13. Who crowns Israel with splendor.
14. Who gives strength to the weary.
15. Who removes sleep from my eyes and slumber from my eyelids.

Here is the list that Lea and Archer agreed upon to include in their service and how we translated them to reflect words that matched their *true* understanding of G-d.

1. Who takes sleep from my eyelids.
2. Who made me in the image of G-d.
3. Who made me free.
4. Who made me Yisrael.
5. Who gives Israel Strength.
6. Who crowns Israel with Splendor.
7. Who gave us the commandments and commanded us to deal with the Torah.

That the blessing of *not* being created as a woman didn't make the cut is obvious in this day and age. That blessing is not even used in modern circles and often gets replaced by being made in the "image of G-d." Interestingly, Archer and Lea didn't relate to G-d giving strength, sight, clothing, or physical freedom. They didn't want to take away from human accomplishment or believe in some fantastic unrealistic G-d. I wondered if they felt that way because they were a product of their Ethical Culture schooling. Blessings giving G-d medicinal powers were eliminated. Archer was strong in crafting this list while his older sister was happy to analyze but go along with whatever topic on which he was strident. Their dynamic echoed the dynamic of their mother and father a bit. Perhaps Lea and Archer were repeating the pattern of their parents. As an educator, it also seemed like we were doing something groundbreaking. To ensure their service would have real relevance, we were writing our own meaningful siddur of prayers that are more than 1,000 years old.

We also cut the *Ashrei,* Psalm 145, all together from their service. Ashrei was the same prayer I sang at my sister's bat mitzvah when I was in the fourth grade. In *Mishnah Brakhot,* the sages discuss that one who learns how to sing the Ashrei secures their place in heaven, or in the world-to-come—the reason being one of the verses reminds us to be generous and provide for the needy.

Talking about this great deed ensures our doing it and deserves a spot in heaven.[56] A rather long psalm of twenty-four verses, with authorship credited to King David, the Ashrei is an alphabetic acrostic, implying that G-d is to be praised for everything. Ashrei literally means happy. "Happy are those who are with G-d . . ." was immediately problematic for my students. First of all, they felt like not everyone who follows G-d or who is Jewish is *happy*. As we were debating all of these prayers, we were in the midst of a tense election cycle and New York Jews were pessimistic about rising anti-Israel feelings and antisemitism. Donald Trump's multiple impeachments and re-election campaign had Upper West Side liberal Jews in a pretzel. Pair all of that with regular preteen angst. The kids didn't feel happy-go-lucky or Pollyanna-ish about G-d. The words of this psalm were off-putting and so we left it out. As a teacher, I had another motive in putting this on the chopping block. While the kids would learn this prayer with transliteration, I knew that the syllables in Hebrew were incredibly hard to sound out. I was concerned that the Ashrei would take up a lot of time in our learning and practicing. I offered the option of only including the verses of the psalm that resonated with them, but because we agreed the thing that made Ashrei special was there was a praise for every letter, it didn't make sense to truncate or alter it. We therefore decided as a team to omit that prayer as well.

The process of studying their Torah portion was the easiest of all. We started learning the proper portion for the day and week of their scheduled service with transliterated Hebrew. Their service was being planned for June of 2020 in Israel. Since 2011, nearly every March and June I've gone to Israel to lead bar and bat mitzvahs. Even before I was an ordained rabbi, I went as the

56 Schwartz, David. n.d. "Ashrei - A Guaranteed Spot in Heaven?" Sefaria. Accessed January 22, 2024. https://www.sefaria.org/sheets/354319?lang=he.

trusted teacher and helped lead the service as a lay-cantor or *shaliach tzibbur,* a public emissary. Now as a rabbi, I was going to lead this family's service somewhere by a kibbutz in the Golan Heights. The Golan is a strategic area in the north of Israel. Beautiful and lush, referenced many times in the Bible, it was recaptured by Israel in the 1967 war. David had visited there and even volunteered with the Israeli Army in his youth. The Six-Day War was an incredible signal to the Jewish people that they were strong and that Israel's army could take a multi-front defensive war and turn it into victory. Having their children's b'nai mitzvah there, looking out over Israel and her neighboring enemy countries, would be sure to inspire Zionism deep inside Archer and Lea.

For this cohort, the Torah's complex cantillation system was unnecessary to stringently decode. The Torah has a singsong way of chanting, so I color coded similar sounding words and tunes. I wrote out the transliteration of nineteen verses and divided them, ten for Archer, and nine for Lea. Archer's ten verses were technically easier than Lea's nine verses. The children would break up and have fifteen minutes of solo time with me during every session and we'd learn one to two more verses in their own section. But the fun part was to analyze the Torah all together. We did many projects as well—hamantaschen baking and latkes on a hotplate when the gas wasn't working in their New York City building. We were on track for a great b'nai mitzvah in Israel.

Three months before their service in Israel, everything in the world changed. The first week of March 2020, New York City was under mandatory lockdown. Israel actually shutdown first. Everything was now up in the air. *Was the world ending? Would we catch a virus and die? Would the kids even make it to their b'nai mitzvah anywhere in the world?* I could no longer see them in person and I had to figure out FaceTime, Skype, and Zoom lessons quickly. *How would we share our materials digitally that all had my hand written notations? How could we sing at the same time if Zoom doesn't allow two participants to speak simultaneously? How were our dogs? Where would we get toilet paper? Where was G-d?* There were so many unknowns and I felt terrible as their provider that I didn't just have the answer.

The parents decided that they would do a b'nai mitzvah service in Telluride, Colorado in August. Their grandparents lived in Telluride and it was one of their favorite family places in the United States. They had to substitute the Rocky Mountains for the mountains of Israel. They offered to fly me out to Colorado to lead the service and arrange for lodging. While they would take a family road trip, given the pandemic, the flights and hotels were actually pretty cheap. I felt comfortable traveling to Colorado either way. News started to reflect that planes were safe, especially if you wore an N95 mask—of which I had two. At the last minute, Elizabeth, as a doctor, began to think about the likelihood of me contracting COVID during my travels and didn't want that on her conscience. She was spooked enough for me to lead the service virtually from my apartment via Zoom.

We set up for one of the weirdest experiences ever. I had led small events that were broadcast via Zoom, even performed a wedding via Zoom, but now, I had to lead and sing with children in another time zone via Zoom. I advised them on sound, room, and lighting setup, but from out of state. I advised them on extension cords, Wi-Fi extenders, and more but without the ability to fast track, control, or really provide a luxury experience. The family borrowed a community Torah scroll, but even that was abnormal. There are different types of scrolls for different ethnic backgrounds of Jews. No matter what, a Torah has no page numbers; a trained person is needed to help roll and find the appropriate portion for the weekly reading, especially if the Torah isn't in the right place. European/Ashkenazi Jews use a Torah scroll about thirty inches long on a podium or table. Sephardic Jews read the Torah standing up in a metal casing. The scroll we borrowed was stuck in a wooden box—like a coffin—and difficult to roll; it also came to us in the completely wrong place in the Five Books of Moses. Through a pointed cell phone on FaceTime, I had to scan column after column and then instruct the family how to find the right place in the scroll so that the children would be able to find their place in the text.

The actual service worked out great. I had prepared custom printed prayer books with all their prayers in the right order, and assigned roles to each of their attending relatives. I shared the screen as I led and the participants had the booklet in hand in Colorado. From New York, I had to tell people when to rise and when to sit, when to come forward, and how to speak in the digital microphones. So that the guests on Zoom could hear properly, I was muting and unmuting like crazy. Plenty of people from the East Coast viewed the service and there were about twelve people present in person. The children did an excellent job and seemed unflustered. I cannot remember any huge glitches. My favorite part of the ceremony was when I would insist the parents or aunts and uncles to do things with the Torah that I would have otherwise done. It really took the entire family to make a mitzvah service, not unlike the way it takes so many hands to raise children. Everyone was so proud of themselves and their children.

There was a huge let down as soon as the service was over. I closed my laptop and that was it. I was so sad to be alone in my apartment by myself, unable to reach out and hug the family to celebrate their accomplishments. I had little control over the energy in the room of the service and I was disappointed that I couldn't gauge their feelings either. I missed the feeling of community. None of my New York network was there, and would never comprehend how nuts it was to pull off a Zoom double bar mitzvah from far away at my dining room table. I was left feeling grateful for Zoom and the internet but sad and alone again, due to the pandemic. I worried that these children wouldn't get a trip to Israel for many years because of the pandemic, college prep, and high school. Other priorities in life could compete for their vacation dollars and time. I worried that because they had such a let down from their initial hopes and dreams from their most formative religious experience, they would never feel really religious. I hoped that their religious or spiritual highpoint could come when they get married or have children. I worried that statistically they may not mark those moments within the Jewish tradition. I do know that they studied hard and felt accomplished.

For a few years now, I've maintained a friendship with David. Especially during the pandemic's dark times, we exchanged article recommendations and asked what the other thought about Jewish current events. I continue to learn from him as an intellectual and enjoy our differences in opinion. I will always remember David's speech he gave at the ceremony to his children. Most of the services I lead, the mother gives a speech during the service and the dad during the party—it's just the way things have worked out. I enjoyed and appreciated David's words, in part because I was present and listening alone in my apartment on Zoom. They are presented below and accompanied by a final paragraph from Elizabeth.

Lea. Archer. Well done.

A b'nai mitzvah in the middle of a global pandemic.

We had a Plan A. You guys were executing that plan. Regular studies with Rabbi Becky and Scout the wonderdog. A great cultural and educational trip planned to Israel. And then, the world changed on a dime. Raging uncertainty gave rise to isolation, and questions swirled about what the future may hold for your b'nai mitzvah . . . and everything else for that matter.

Without much of a hitch, you both transitioned to Plan B and wonderfully performed your ceremony today. As you look around, you're in as beautiful a place as exists on this planet as described by your Grandpa Art. Moreover, you're surrounded by family and friends, in person and virtually, who love you and are thrilled by your achievements. While the journey was quite different than anticipated, the destination is clearly pretty sweet. Along the way to this date . . . and having sat in on several of your sessions . . . I know that you learned a lot about what it means to be a Jew today, how the media shapes policy, and the thorny, seemingly unsolvable issues that plague modern-day Israel.

As this rite of passage marks your induction into adulthood, perhaps this complicated backdrop of a pandemic and an election and Black Lives Matter is the perfect welcome mat to what we adults all know—we really don't know a lot. There's an old Yiddish adage that goes "Mann tracht, un Gott lacht," or "man plans and G-d laughs." What we do *know is that if you don't make a plan, you ain't going anywhere.*

And let me tell you, Lea and Archer, you guys are going places. How do I know? Having had a front row seat at your lives from day one, we've heard ambitions ranging from fireman, cosmetic dentist, pig, architect, rockologist, and teacher, to name a few. And while dreams are wonderful, you both possess the goods to realize your dreams, whatever they may be.

Here, I'm reminded of the three-legged stool of success. If you have two components, great but you're still going to fall over. Success requires all three. The first necessary condition is a willingness to work hard. The effort has nothing to do with ability and everything to do with dedication and work ethic. Whether it's twenty hours per week in the gym, squash lessons for forty-five minutes in the middle of a pandemic, late-night studying for school, or endless Spanish flash cards in preparation for an exam, investing yourself in your craft is a seemingly innate ability for each of you.

The second leg of the stool is knowing yourself. As you get older, you trust that little voice within you, unswayed by the opinions of others. For some people, it can take a lifetime to feel comfortable in their own skin. For others, well, it seems to occur at birth. How else do you explain being the slowest walker, dresser, eater, teeth brusher in Manhattan despite the constant exhortations to move faster? Or finding expression through mismatched socks, bucket hats, terrible rap music, and the color pink? As much as I tease you both about your adolescent prefrontal lobe circuitry, your grasp of abstract ideas and your ability to interact with an array of people belies your age. I love watching your personalities develop and I love chatting you up on the topic of the day not only because you generally have something intelligent to say but mostly because you say it in your own, distinct voice.

The last element of the three-legged stool is grit, that ability to adjust and persevere in the face of unforeseen challenges. If things like pandemics wouldn't occur, I guess you could stick with just the first two traits, but that ain't how life works. And no, not everything will be as dramatic as a global, unstoppable virus. That said, you've both overcome some significant obstacles in your young lives with grace and resolve. Lea, it's hard to imagine the daily cesspool of abusive gymnastics instruction you endured for years. Not only did you figure out how to separate your love of the sport from the actions of a few demented coaches, you're now four years beyond those days, excelling, and most importantly, enjoying the process. You've accomplished something few others could even contemplate. Archer, you too were singled out. Through no fault of your own, your super-woke school targeted you and leveled baseless accusations. You grew up a lot, adjusted your behavior, and interestingly, had your best academic year to date. *You even said recently that you were grateful for the experience.*

As much as Mom and I lament the loss of your innocence, we beam with pride as you develop the inner strength to handle the curveballs that life may throw your way. No longer will we see a one-year-old vintage Lea unapologetically and relentlessly screaming for pretzels in the back of a cab from O'Hare with Grammy Boo or a two-year-old vintage Archer going full-on Exorcist at 90 Prince St. after a long day of traveling in the car. Today's versions are more measured, thoughtful. And yet, as your goals crystallize and you begin planning how to achieve them, don't forget about that part of you that found such joy in barreling down a vault runway at the World's competition in Florida or touching the caboose in a school of fish in the Galapagos. Mazel tov!

Elizabeth: *Before we end this part of your special day, I want both of you to take note of how fortunate you are and know there are always those less fortunate than you. Now that you enter adulthood, remember it is our responsibility to reach out to those less fortunate and lend a hand. Whether building a house for poor folks in Guatemala, chatting with a lonely elder, or helping serve and deliver food during COVID-19 to those who can't afford a meal, please always find it in your heart to be generous and kind.*

We love you!

Never-ending are the lessons from the way this family decided to approach their children's education. I decided to include them in this collection of stories to demonstrate thoughtful parenting, with space for children to fully develop their own beliefs. It is clear that David had strong opinions, but he let his children form their own. Having vision for the way you want to raise your family, and what values you want to highlight takes tons of reinforcement;

the type of school you send your kids to, the type of rabbi or Jewish community you choose, and even the place in Israel you decide to have your bar mitzvah service. What is clear is that you do not need to believe in G-d in order to raise your kids with love of Judaism and Jewish values. You don't need to believe in G-d in order to participate in the rituals of our people or to feel a sense of belonging. This is extremely important to understand with emerging statistics from Pew that show twenty-eight percent of Americans report to be "nones" or of no religious affiliation.[57] As a rabbi, I am proud of my own ability to be flexible and meet the needs of those in front of me. I grew as a result of serving this family that would have been otherwise lost and disengaged from Jewish study. Years later, Lea and I had a text conversation about keeping kosher as a way to stay active and proud of Jewish practices and as she heads off to her first year of college, no doubt, she will experience a whole different subset of peers and face inevitable antisemitism. All the time, I meet de-shuled people who say they miss being in a Jewish community but a certain life circumstance or tragedy caused them to lose belief in G-d. I remind them they do not have to believe in order to practice or partake, and I try to invite them in. In this day and age, we need leaders who hold space for those who question and wrestle. After all, that is the meaning of the term "Israel," to wrestle with G-d.

---

57 Mandler, C. 2024. "More than 1 in 4 U.S. Adults Identify as Religious 'Nones,' New Data Shows. Here's What This Means." *CBS NEWS*, January 24, 2024. https://www.cbsnews.com/news/religious-nones-more-than-1-in-4-u-s-adults-pew-research-center-report/.

CONFESSION VII:
Israel is the Jewish homeland, but for those who consider it home, it's a lot more complicated.

"I knew all along that I could not escape Jerusalem: her contrasts, conflicts, and contradictions are my own internal landscape."
—HISTORIAN MERON BENVENISTI,
DEPUTY MAYOR OF JERUSALEM 1971 – 1978[58]

Case study 4

Some families have a giant family portrait over their fireplace or in the center of their gallery wall. I grew up idolizing an old photo of my mother from 1974, blown up and hung in the center of the family room. It was of her, on the last day of her first trip to Israel, with the famous Israeli General Moshe Dayan. He had recently resigned as minister of defense under Golda Meir's administration. Dayan, born in 1915 during the Ottoman Empire in Kibbutz Degania Alef (which was Ottoman-Syria), became a leader in the Haganah defense forces prior to the establishment of Israel in 1948. He was a commander through the War of Independence and many other defensive wars Israel fought in her first decades as a young and vulnerable country. In 1967, during the Six-Day War, under his military leadership, Israel recaptured

---

58 Benvenisti, Meron. 1988. "TWO GENERATIONS: GROWING UP IN JERUSALEM." The *New York Times,* October 16, 1988. https://www.nytimes.com/1988/10/16/magazine/two-generations-growing-up-in-jerusalem.html.

Jerusalem from Jordan. Recognizable for wearing an eye patch, he became the symbol for Israel's military strength and victory. Up until the Yom Kippur War in 1973, he was included in nearly every Israeli government cabinet and was considered a candidate for prime minister. The multiple failures of intelligence that lead to heavy casualties during the 1973 war supposedly deeply depressed Dayan and he went off the grid for some time after. My mother ran into him at an antique shop in Jerusalem. He was infamous for his archeological artifacts collection—many of which came into question for their legality by the Israeli Antiquities Authority. My mother had no doubt that it was her hero, the man responsible for the borders of Israel post 1967. A smiling blonde American in awe of one of Israel's founding fathers, she snapped a shot with the last film on her role. Forever we'd look at that photo as a symbol of my mom's appreciation for the early leaders of Israel, their sacrifice and heroism, and our connection to them. We never openly talked about his controversial collection of historical stolen artifacts or about how he himself admitted, under his military leadership, in 1973 Israel came close to the destruction of the third temple—meaning losing the entire country. Like many center-right leaning American Jews, we would neglect to mention that he belonged to center-left political parties and was in favor of coexistence with Palestinians and Israelis in one singular country with equal rights for all.

The Dayan family to Israel is like the Kennedy family to America. His first wife, Ruth Dayan, was the celebrated fashion company founder of Maskit, a clothing brand for women that purposefully employed female immigrants. Moshe Dayan's daughter, Yael Dayan, was a respected Israeli Knesset member and author. His sons were Udi, a sculptor, and Assi, a film director and actor. While Dayan lost popularity during the Yom Kippur War, the Dayan family was still famous, always in the news, and the generation of grandchildren include pop-rock star Aviv Geffen.

In Jerusalem, in June of 2018, I met Dayan's granddaughter, Amalia Dayan, a renowned art dealer and gallerist. She and her family were attending the bat mitzvah of Phoebe Rice, the daughter of Julie Rice, cofounder of SoulCycle, and at the time chief branding officer of WeWork (during the tremendous time up, before the crash). I knew that Amalia was coming to the bat mitzvah but I had no idea that she would be this elegant woman. She had the effortless beauty of a European model, and if you squinted, she carried the face of her grandfather. I was starstruck. Now just a digital scan that resided in my iPhone, I showed her the picture of my mom with her grandfather that I kept in my "favorites" album. While she was incredibly gracious to listen, she seemed completely indifferent and detached from the photo.

Even though her girls had an Israeli mother, Amalia's daughters, Zohar and Noa, were raised on the Upper East Side of Manhattan. Their conversational Hebrew language skills were from lessons on the computer with a teacher I'd never met. The family's religious involvement was not consistent before Phoebe's bat mitzvah. Israel, the holy land, is actually about fifty percent secular. Only a quarter of the population of Israel is strictly religious and the other quarter of Israel's population is not even Jewish![59] Most Israelis feel that their religion is being Israeli, and speaking Hebrew is the way to exercise their Judaism. Built into Israeli culture are Friday night dinners, religious governmental holidays, and the scarcity of non-kosher food. While the religious and traditional Jews maintain the authority over nearly all religious institutions in Israel, clearly the majority of Israelis are secular and feel sufficiently religious just through the structure of their society. The extended Dayan family was a-religious and left

---

59 Jewish Virtual Library, a project of The American-Israeli Cooperative Enterprise. 2024. "Vital Statistics: Latest Population Statistics for Israel." https://www.jewishvirtuallibrary.org/latest-population-statistics-for-israel.

leaning. Typically, religious people are more right-wing in Israel. No matter if you are right or left, it is extremely rare in Israel for a girl to read from the Torah, even at a bat mitzvah ceremony. That is not allowed in religious circles. Moreover, in secular communities it is simply viewed as unimportant. Zohar and Noa's Hebrew Zoom schooling was more of a way to learn to communicate when they would spend time with their great-grandmother Ruth, great aunt Yael, or other family in Israel.

The story goes that Amalia, who worked in art dealing, visited an art exhibit, when Adam Lindemann walked up to her and told her she was the most beautiful thing in the whole gallery. Their 2006 Jerusalem wedding is still listed in an online *Vogue* article as one of the "most beautiful social weddings of all time."[60] Adam and Amalia fell in love and created a family together. Adam was culturally Jewish, having grown up in the Reform movement. He was a former renowned polo player and celebrated art collector. Adam happened to be an excellent musician and had a unique love for the guitar and banjo. They both loved the beach, education, the finer things, and their children. Amalia loved Adam's three older daughters and raised her daughters to consider them as full sisters. Adam was at times moody but it was nothing Amalia's grace couldn't handle.

After the Rice's service (at a privately rented spot of the Southern Temple Wall at the Davidson Center in Jerusalem), Zohar was interested in also becoming a bat mitzvah. It made complete sense to me. Here she was, in her maternal homeland, in the city for which her great-grandfather led the capture and victory, and she was hearing all songs in her mother's tongue and watching a ritual being led by a fun female rabbi who idolized her

---

60 Van Zanten, Virginia. 2015. "The Most Beautiful Social Weddings of All Time." *Vogue*, December 22, 2015. https://www.vogue.com/article/most-beautiful-social-weddings-kennedy-bessette-bush.

family. Everyone participated happily and proudly in this service. Zohar wanted to be a part of this tradition. The Rice and Lindemann families continued their beautiful friendships with Shabbat dinners, holiday celebrations, and New York socializing. Zohar went to a very competitive school in the Upper East Side and probably started to hear about young girls studying Hebrew for their bat mitzvahs. I finally got a message from Amalia that Zohar was ready to start bat mitzvah training in the summer of 2019.

In my first session with Zohar, I remember sitting in her family's extraordinary home in Montauk, the former estate of Andy Warhol. After a long drive east from where I stayed in Bridgehampton, I followed a long private entrance with gates, codes, and security. Finally, I entered into a property with several cottages and a large main house that sits on the cliff overlooking the edge of North America. It has the most beautiful quiet beach with waves lapping at the rocky Montauk shore. I felt like a pilgrim having just discovered the coast of a country. Out bounced a tanned, smiling young girl not wearing shoes, like a typical kibbutz kid of Israel. Zohar greeted me sweetly and said she wanted to do her lesson at one of the outdoor areas by a table. Armed with Israeli candy to motivate her, our lesson stretched for more than an hour and didn't require chocolate to keep her interest. Plus, Zohar was already familiar with these brands of chocolate and far preferred Swiss or boutique organic brands. Zohar went through an entire book of Hebrew letters in one sitting. We spot-checked her reading. We read words and talked about the meaning of religious phrases. It was so interesting, because she was literate in Hebrew but completely illiterate in our religion. She did not know why we celebrate the Sabbath rest day (to mark creation weekly and to remember liberation from slavery in Egypt). She had never heard the story of creation or of the Garden of Eden. She did not know a single prayer, or even the basic combination of

"Baruch atah Adonai," "Blessed are you, our Eternal G-d." In some ways, we were starting from an advanced position and in other ways, at the total beginning. Because we were doing something for the first time, I taught her the *Shehecheyanu* blessing, a prayer thanking G-d for sustaining us and reaching this moment in time, said the first time doing something or the first day of a holiday period. It was her homework to practice. Like the rest of her assignments, Zohar would take this deeply to her heart.

Zohar wanted her bat mitzvah to be held in Jerusalem at the same Sephardic synagogue where her parents got married. While Amalia had an effortless style, she had intentionality behind every detail. Right before sunset, we'd close down the beautiful synagogue to invite guests for cocktails; then we'd hold a private prayer service led by me and Zohar; then they'd throw a party at another fabulous location nearby. To be honest, the whole order of things made me nervous. *Would a synagogue in Jerusalem allow me, a nondenominational female rabbi from New York, to lead a bat mitzvah service, including a Torah reading?* In Israel, in a religious setting, women are not permitted to even sing in crowds where men are present. Women are not accepted as rabbis. (That female clergy are accepted in America is because the majority of American Jews abide by the rules of the Reform or Conservative movements. In Israel they are the minority). Even though Amalia was not religious, I believe she knew this and it slipped her mind. She had been living in the states for more than twenty-five years. Besides that, she was used to planning fabulous events and making her dreams a reality. I don't think she saw how difficult it was to pull off her vision. At the same time, Amalia was following in the footsteps of her family members and making a deliberate choice by having a female rabbi lead a service for her daughter to read from the Torah. She was thereby expressing her liberal views towards religion, her frustration with the place of women, and the opinion that women should have the ability to lead religious services whenever and wherever. She hired Ofer Gover and Tali Yaacobi, the best Israeli party planners, to pull off the lavish, detailed, and extraordinary events. Zohar's bat mitzvah was scheduled for June of 2020.

Half way into the planning, COVID-19 hit. Zohar had made great progress and learned many prayers, Torah stories, and was nearly finished with her Torah reading about Korah, Moses's rebellious cousin. However, like many New Yorkers, Zohar's family moved almost full time to Montauk and lessons stopped for a few months. The trip to Israel was canceled. As the plans started to firm up again, we realized that COVID variants, testing, masks, and travel restrictions were all still a consideration months later. As a family, the Lindemanns decided to host Zohar's bat mitzvah celebration one year later in June of 2021 in Montauk. Their younger daughter would hopefully be the reason to bring the whole family together in Israel in 2022.

In the fall of 2020, Zohar picked up learning once again. During the #MeToo movement, watching Zohar and her little sister Noa find their voices was really meaningful. They idolized their three brilliant older sisters and appreciated them as role models. Zohar had quotes from famous female poets hung on her wall. She was light, charming, and supportive. She spoke only after pausing, tilting her head and eyes, and after carefully considering what she would say. She was a little spacey and would never know where her materials were, but I couldn't blame her because she didn't concern herself with material items. Being one of the great-grandchildren of Moshe Dayan didn't really interest her as much as being related to her formidable grandmother Frayda B. Lindemann, president of the Metropolitan Opera. Grandma Lindemann was elegant and warm. She raised her family in the classiest of ways. I remember when Grandma Lindemann gave Zohar a pair of gold earrings for her twelfth birthday that I thought were so beautiful and notably sophisticated. The love of music that permeated the children was obviously passed down through Grandma Lindemann.

Adam, who would endlessly play banjo in his study, had gotten more mercurial since COVID-19. That proved a challenge for me and his daughters to navigate. I was no stranger to demanding clients, but Adam was scary sometimes. His sense of humor was tough, and he'd say strong statements like "get that dog out of my house" or "no wonder no one wants to marry you, Becky." I realized this was his way of joking with me and that Adam really loved me. So, I could get through the off-color comments and also manage when he and his daughters would spar. For example, Adam repeatedly shared a story of his disgraced childhood rabbi being "me too-ed," or fired from his position as rabbi due to sexual misconduct with a minor.[61] That rabbi has since been stripped of all of his titles by the Union of Reform Judaism. Zohar always responded strongly to her dad that his childhood rabbi was the predator, not the "me too" victim. I found this typical clash between adolescent daughter and conservative father familiar to my own.

Adam also insisted on playing guitar to accompany both daughters during their prayer services. Orthodox services do not use musical instruments, but in New York City, some synagogues use an organ or employ a full orchestral band. During the two months leading up to the bat mitzvah, we held rehearsal sessions in the family kitchen. I had to play music director and referee. My pastoral counseling and performance background were needed at

---

61   Elia-Shalev, Asaf. 2023. "Disgraced Former Reform Movement Leader Sheldon Zimmerman Expelled from Rabbinical Association." *Jewish Telegraphic Agency*, February 14, 2023. https://www.jta.org/2023/02/14/united-states/disgraced-former-reform-movement-leader-sheldon-zimmerman-expelled-from-rabbinical-association.

the same time. Adam wanted his daughter to sing perfectly and powerfully. I wanted the words and the feeling of a prayer to be right. I needed Adam to practice his sheet music. He would often say, "who wrote this crap?" about the well-respected melodies used by the Reform and Conservative movements. He would also say, "I don't know this song," as if it was an excuse to not play. I'd tell him to learn it. He was actually excellent. I loved the drama and watching him go from combative to interested, engaged and in-sync with his daughter. When he didn't lead clearly or added too many embellishments, I'd remind him about his goal: "You're here to help Zohar find the notes and sing these prayers." I'd instruct and then he really adjusted; it was like a metaphoric lesson in parenting. Sometimes Adam would stop and remind Zohar of how exquisite her singing was and the moment was very tender. Somehow, with a lot of rehearsal, patience, and authority, we pulled it off and bonded in a deeper way. Adam actually did a great job and supported Zohar with his talents. I joked that I would book him to accompany other children at future gigs.

Throughout the entire duration of planning Zohar's service, the only conflict I had with Amalia was how to handle the Prayer for the State of Israel. At first, this surprised me because she was from such a prominent Israeli family. After leaving Israel to obtain a master's degree at the age of twenty-four, and after many decades living in New York City, Amalia still had a strong Israeli accent. Initially, I knew very little about the historic family's personal lives and political leanings. Over time, I realized that her seeming distance from Dayan history had more to do with carving out her independent identity. She never bit when I talked about her family unless it was about the women. While famous and respected, Amalia's father and grandfather had public scandals and moral failings that were widely reported. Instead, Amalia had a strong relationship with her mother, Aharona Melnick; her grandmother

Ruth Dayan; and Aunt, Yael Dayan. During one of my first family dinners in Montauk, I remember Adam telling me about Amalia's Israeli family and their beliefs. I learned that the family believed the establishment of the State of Israel had less to do with the Holocaust and more with global antisemitism. The Dayan family had been living under British mandate for decades prior to 1948; they developed barren land as their only escape from age-old European Jew-hate. For them, Israel's statehood was the result of a 2,000-year-old need to return to an ancestral homeland, not just the world's guilt from the Holocaust. At the age of 103, Ruth Dayan passed away a few months before Zohar's ceremony. As we read the obituaries, Zohar shared the memories of visiting her great-grandmother's eclectically decorated home in Tel Aviv. I would later learn that Amalia's dear aunt, Yael Dayan, was a Knesset member for eleven years from 1992–2003, mostly as a member of the Labor Party. She was a believer in peace and a two-state solution, LGBTQ+ rights, women's advancement, and advocacy for victims of sexual harassment. Still, Amalia rarely opined when it came to Israel's government. Like many people living outside their birth country, Amalia did not serve in any political capacity. Furthermore, the Israeli political scene is incredibly divisive even among Jews, and we were just coming off of a violent conflict in Gaza in the spring of 2021. At the time, Amalia did not agree with some of the choices Israel had made, but she didn't share specifics. Amalia believed in having only peaceful, non-divisive language at her daughter's ceremony. She did not want to offer a prayer for the State of Israel, and because she was previously secular and unfamiliar with religious services, she was unfamiliar that the Israel prayer was even a part of our liturgy. To me this was more than complicated. I had met this family in Israel and the girls were half Israeli. To me, Amalia was, by extension, a symbol of the founding fathers of Israel. Then again, we were using so many other parts of Zohar's bat mitzvah as creative expressions of our Judaism. The family was decidedly not traditional. So how could I hold so fastidiously to this moment of a prayer for Israel? As a compromise, we agreed that I would invite the congregation to turn eastward, towards the shore of the Atlantic Ocean, and encourage everyone to offer their heartfelt prayers towards Israel in silence in whatever way they felt so moved. If only all compromises concerning Israel could be reached that easily.

It could be due to the great reviews from Zohar's service, or the fact that I was the only person who could handle the many facets of this family, that I was instantly on a schedule for Noa's training and bat mitzvah lessons. Noa was a totally different student from Zohar. Noa was sassy and a pistol. She was a therapist in training. Noa was Zohar's best friend, but also *everyone else's* best friend. At times I felt like she was my best friend, too. I told Noa how I'd broken up with the boyfriend I brought to Zohar's service because he told me to freeze my eggs. Noa told me that someone she knew was freezing their eggs and it inspired her that women take control of their own destinies and didn't have to rely on men. She articulated that it was beautiful that women no longer have to be "chosen" to become someone's wife to be a mother. A week later I made an appointment to freeze my eggs and go on my own fertility journey. I would have never done it without Noa's encouragement and support.

It was a family decision that Noa, the youngest great-granddaughter of Moshe Dayan, would be the only Lindemann to have her bat mitzvah in Israel. On an epic four-day trip to Tel Aviv with 100 of the family's closest friends and clients, we would usher Noa into womanhood on the beach of Jaffa. In front of the Peres Center for Peace and Innovation, named after Shimon Peres, the former visionary president of Israel, we'd sing prayers with the sunset kissing our backs and the waves of the Mediterranean lapping at the shores of our homeland. As poetic as something Zohar would write, the congregation would watch Noa and look off to the horizon simultaneously, symbolizing her future and Judaism meeting in this magical place. With musical moments of the service accompanied either by Noa's father, Adam, or by Israeli Rock legend and relative Aviv Geffen, this service was like none other. What could be better? Family and friends had flown in from everywhere and overtaken Tel Aviv hotels. Some of the world's most successful people were in attendance. I was even allowed to invite a plus one and choose my friend Aaron Gelbman, one of my best friends from college, who had made Aliyah years prior. After feeling shut in after years of the COVID-19 lockdown, the airy setup on the beach between the ancient port of Jaffa and modern Tel Aviv seemed so refreshing and right. There was a sense of freedom and joy that whole week. Noa and her family would be hard to nail down between lunches and surfing trips. They were completely carefree Israelis *and* polished socialites. Noa's oldest then-living Israeli relative, her aunt Yael, was in attendance for both the welcome dinner at the Tel Aviv Museum of Art and the ceremony. Yael looked exactly like her father, Moshe Dayan. I went up to her and spoke with her in Hebrew. She had a breathing apparatus, and could not speak. She nodded her head gracefully and I truly felt like I was in the presence of greatness.

Being in Israel with Amalia, I started to understand her conflicted Israeli identity. I observed Amalia in a new light that took me months to unpack. Unlike the anonymity she had in New York, she could not escape being a Dayan. But to Amalia, being a Dayan was about being a person of integrity, not about being a symbol of Israel. People are complex and nuanced. Once someone comes face-to-face with the humanity within their family it changes their sense of reality; this is much more amplified when someone understands that a hero or country is flawed. I never heard Amalia criticize Israel or her country's policies, but I sensed something. You see, typical Israelis boast with pride about their national identity and Amalia was very private. I think, for Amalia, facing the human flaws of her personal patriarchy led to her own disengagement from the historic identity of her family and her country. She understood how the sausage was made, and she wanted a break from the factory. Israel was not The Promised Land; Israel was her home country. What would keep her coming back was her relatives and role models in Ruth and Yael Dayan who often pushed Israel towards a more progressive future. But like everyone has to accept that their family has their issues, Amalia deeply felt Israel had her's. For many who find a flaw and disengage, it is really hard to bring them back into the fold. Life cycle moments of her wedding and the bat mitzvah in Israel kept the channel open.

It was no surprise that at Noa's bat mitzvah the tension returned around how to handle the Prayer for the State of Israel. Even though times were different, Amalia was firm and did not want to use the typical liturgy. As a compromise, with relatively little debate, Amalia decided that she would ask her cousin, Rachel, to read a poem or psalm. Rachel read the Hebrew text of Psalm 121 in slow and authentic Hebrew. The first sentence translates to: "I lift up my eyes up to the hills, from where does my help come? My help comes from G-d, who has made heaven and earth." It was a beautiful reading and that reflected the ability to be flexible for all.

Contrast that compromise with the rigidity of the Torah reading cycle. The way the Jewish religion dictates which story of the Torah is to be read is very straightforward; we follow a weekly cycle and go in order of sections to complete the entire reading of the Torah within one year. Simchat Torah, which is observed twenty-two days after the Jewish New Year (usually in

September), is when we complete and then restart the Torah scroll. Typically, a child having a bar or bat mitzvah schedules their event close to their birthday and the date automatically corresponds with a proper Torah portion. A child will learn to chant at least a couple of verses of the portion, if not the whole reading. It is a beautiful thought that no matter where you are in the world, on most Sabbaths, everywhere in the world Jewish people are on the same "page," or column, of the Torah, learning and relearning the same stories and lessons. But I was suggesting something different. Because the COVID-19 pandemic had wreaked havoc on so many events with scheduling and rescheduling, I would sometimes suggest that a child learn the Torah portion that corresponded with a child's birthday according to the Jewish lunar calendar; that day and portion almost always does not correspond to the same date or portion on the Gregorian calendar every year. There is a way to look up what Torah portion corresponds with a birth-date. That portion is part of their destiny, and often in Orthodox circles is how a bar or bat mitzvah is scheduled in the first place. But after COVID-19, I became very flexible about choosing a portion. If a birthday portion was significant in some way to the family, I would allow it, even if it would not correspond with the typical reading cycle. I wasn't the first rabbi to come up with this and I found supportive religious reasoning as to why it would still be permissible. During various times in exile Jews have been off schedule and out of sync in their readings. There were traditional rabbis who would make a child learn the proper portion for the date, and in the event of a date change, a child had to master a whole new set of complicated Hebrew verses. I have always cared more about the meaning behind our choices and about how much fun a child has during their preparation for their big day. I think it's terrible to add anxiety that at any moment they may have to learn something else or what they are learning won't be relevant.

That will not leave a child with a positive feeling about becoming a Jewish adult or encourage them to continue Jewish practice.

Noa decided she wanted to learn the Torah portion in which the character "Noa" appears. Noa is one of the most popular names in Israel. Contrary to the belief that this is the female version of Noah, with the flood and the ark in Genesis, Noa is actually a separate figure in the scripture; she and her sisters advocate for their inheritance when their father dies without a male heir. In the Book of Numbers, Noa is often looked at as a feminist leader, fighting for her rightful portion. She changed the Jewish law due to her argument. It's no wonder that secular Israelis would name their daughters Noa. Liberal Israelis (like the Dayans) empower women to achieve just as much as men and encourage their daughters to do as much as they want in the world. Noa loved learning the story and relating it back to all the women in her life. Her speech below reflects that learning:

Hello and thank you all for being here. When choosing a Torah portion to read for my bat mitzvah, I was interested in learning about the Torah character Noa, whom I was named after. It is a pretty popular name in Israel, and obviously my mom's favorite name Zohar, was already taken by my older sister. Noa is one of five sisters . . . hmmm sounds familiar. She is brave and advocates for herself and for her family. Let me tell you what happened:

Noa's father is named Tzelophad. Okay . . . similarities between our worlds are running out. Tzelophchad had no sons. He dies with no male heir. According to Israelite law, all his assets and property were being given to other male members of his family and the daughters were supposed to be left with nothing. In my portion, they decide to stand up for themselves and take the terrifying walk to the tabernacle to plead with Moshe, Eleazar the priest, and the other chieftains. They approach Moshe and explain that their father died, but wasn't a part of a big rebellion against Moshe and Aaron. For those of you that were at Zohar's bat mitzvah, that was her portion. Tzelophchad was imperfect but not guilty of this terrible uprising. The five daughters point out that Tzelophcad's name doesn't deserve to die out along with him. They deserve to receive a portion of his land and inheritance. Moshe takes the matter up with G-d. G-d agrees that it is only just to let them have a piece of Tzelophchad's inheritance. G-d also changes the laws moving forward. If a man has no sons to inherit his property, his daughters should inherit. If he has no daughters, then his brothers inherit. The part of this story that I find most interesting and challenging is the fact that the five daughters had the confidence to speak to Moshe. This came after a long history of women not having agency or ability.

It is also very inspiring how the five sisters were all united in this appeal.

In Hebrew it first says "Vah-Tik-Ravana." They came forward as a group of nameless daughters. Then, later in the sentence, the daughters suddenly change; They are named and the Torah recognizes that each of the daughters are individual people with unique names. They are Machlah, Noa, Hoglah, Milkah, and Tirzah. After that list, the Torah says the women stand up before the group of dignitaries. Countless women at this time didn't stand up. But they stood up for their rights. From walking forward to standing up, the daughters are empowered. We know this because the Torah cares to even mention their names. So many daughters and women were never listed. But that subtle detail of listing their names helps us as readers and them as characters feel their power. They are making a change and fighting for what they believe in. This moment shows the real power of sisterhood.

I'm really inspired by these women and I care a lot about women's rights. I try to stand up for myself and for my friends every possible chance I have. Women in 2022 still don't get the same opportunities as men just because of their gender. Women are still looked past and disregarded or have to constantly prove themselves.

When looking for inspiration in my own life I see the example of a few great women, starting with my great-grandmother Ruth Dayan. She was the wife of Moshe Dayan, but she didn't allow herself to just become the "wife." She wasn't nameless, she kept her own identity. In 1954 in Israel, Ruth founded a fashion company called Maskit utilizing traditional craft techniques from Hungarian, Yemenite, Bulgarian, Bedouin, Palestinian, Druze, Lebanese, and Jewish artisans. By creating jobs for these women, she changed their lives as well as started an innovative business. She received several awards for her social activism for women's rights and promoting peace between Arabs and Israelis. She was the most open-minded, accepting person I've ever met. I loved visiting her charming and cultured apartment in Tel Aviv. There were photos everywhere and I would hear stories about who everyone was and adventures from her very full life. Ruth Dayan passed away last year and leaves behind a legacy of courage and success. Another big inspiration in my life is my Grandma Frayda who I am lucky to be able to spend so much time with. I admire my grandma's intelligence, her love and knowledge of music, and her dedication to the performance arts. I also look up to my great aunt Yael who during her career as a parliament member fought rigorously and changed the laws in the field of women's rights, children's rights, LGBTQIA+ rights, and made a real difference. And Andrea, who has been by my side since I was born and with her great values and resilience. I'm lucky to have four sisters. Helen, Charlotte, Frances, and Zohar. Each one is a role model in a different way. Helen, with her care and compassion. Charlotte, with her openness and endless curiosity. Frances, with her originality and creativity. Zohar, for always being true to herself. And last but not least my mom with her dedication, hard work, and drive. Finally, I want to thank my rabbi, Becky, another incredible woman creating your own path in a traditional world is truly admiration-al.

As a bat mitzvah, and young Jewish woman, I know that I will continue on this path. It's a Jewish value to stand up for what's right—and I love that I'm named after such a pioneering and strong spirit.

Working with the Dayan-Lindemann family is one of the highlights of my career. The experience helped me understand the importance we place on symbols as American Jews, living outside of Israel. A family pilgrimage trip to Israel to mark a child's coming of age is an excellent option for so many families—whether de-shuled or affiliated. Ceremonies are almost always held in the holy city of Jerusalem or the ancient military stronghold, Masada. As an American Jew, I hope to mark my future children's special moments at Jerusalem's Western Wall egalitarian prayer platform. But when I view Amalia's thoughtful choices, I see that Israel to Israelis is more than a symbol; it is their home that holds memories. Like everyone, people get frustrated with their places of origin and want to carve a new path for themselves. When Israelis or deeply connected American Jews criticize or suggest reform to Israeli government or law, they aren't being anti-Israel—they see beyond the enormous concept of Israel and recognize it as an ongoing project. I realized that Zohar's Jerusalem venue was chosen not because it was holy or even a synagogue, but because it was personal to Adam and Amalia: it was their wedding venue. I learned that Amalia's deliberate decision to hold a service at the Peres Center for Peace and Innovation was because it was on the shores of her home country, but not too deeply inland. Like the sea's water, there is a flow in identity between who Amalia is now as an Israeli, Upper East Sider, and Montauk surfer. Instead of employing one of my religious musicians, she had her alternative rockstar cousin with a lit cigarette and whiskey drink on the ritual stage. What's more, she passed her strength and vision to her own daughters. Zohar and Noa care that they are linked to a historical family but are very interested in finding out who they are for themselves. They look at the women of their family for inspiration; their warmth and nurturing give life to the otherwise cold militaristic symbol of their great-grandfather. In a modern world, extraordinary people don't just follow and accept symbols. They are on a quest to find and define themselves. Extraordinary and thoughtful people are leaving organized religion hand over fist because many of the symbols no longer speak to their hearts. As a provider, I try to help families find relevance with the rich rituals of Judaism and Israel—even though there is plenty with which to disagree. Simultaneously, I can express gratitude towards the founders, military heroes, and holy sites of Israel while holding personal frustrations towards Israel's Knesset, prime ministers, and the political sway of fringe ultra-religious special interest groups. Being a Jew and lover of Israel is nuanced and I am forever engaged in sharpening my identity and views.

CONFESSION VIII:
Rabbis need to have a personal life.

Case Study 5 (Names have been changed and identities have been obscured or written as a composite characters)

Carrie and Don came to me from someone who had attended a small wedding that I had officiated. They emailed me and asked if I was free on a particular Sunday morning that they had already selected to hold a baby naming ceremony for their sweet daughter, Felice. Even though they now resided in Atlanta, they would travel "home" to New York to hold the event. They had the Brooklyn location, date in April, and brunch hour already decided. All they needed was an officiant who was skilled to bless their daughter according to the Jewish traditions and bestow upon her a Hebrew name.

Traditionally, Jewish baby boys are named at their circumcision ceremony commonly referred to as a *bris*. The ritual is performed by a special type of officiant called a *mohel*, who is certified in this practice. Circumcision is a requirement for all Jewish baby boys. While only a small fraction of Jews no longer circumcise their sons, some Reform or interfaith couples opt to do the procedure in the hospital under the care of a surgeon. In the last seventy-five years, a somewhat common tradition of a baby naming ceremony for Jewish baby girls has emerged among non-Orthodox Jewish circles. Many couples choose to do a *simchat bat*, rejoicing over a daughter ceremony, on either the Shabbat morning a week after or within a few weeks of birth. There is no exact ceremony that must happen. A common custom has emerged during the *aliyot,* blessings and readings over the Torah. After parents recite the blessings over the Torah, the clergy will provide a special *Mi Shebeirach,* blessing, over the child and her parents. I love the way Romemu does this; they place a baby in a tallit and lay it on the Torah scroll, while under a *chupph,* or canopy. The symbolism of an innocent child, wrapped in our tradition and text as they are welcomed into a peaceful canopy at their place of worship is just exquisite.

When a family doesn't belong to a synagogue, they usually choose to make their own ceremony at home or at an event space with a rabbi familiar with the family. But this couple didn't really have that. Carrie and Don scheduled a virtual call with me and I would soon get to know them. As a couple in their late forties, Felice was their first, and most likely, only baby together. Carrie looked like a typical Jewish woman who had just had a baby: no makeup, tired eyes, and a smile. Perhaps what was most striking, and what I was less prepared for, was that Don was actually an Afro-Dominican from the Dominican Republic. For many rabbis, their interfaith relationship would be problematic. I did not have to marry the couple as they had already gotten married during the pandemic. I was not being asked to bless their interfaith marriage. My task was to help name their baby and bless her according to the Jewish traditions.

Interestingly, as I learned more about these two parents, Carrie revealed that her father was Italian. She mentioned being both Jewish and Catholic. However, according to the strictest forms of Jewish Law, Carrie and her baby were still Jewish because they both had Jewish mothers. *Halacha,* Jewish law, dictates that the religious identity is passed through the identity of the mother. I had zero problems blessing this sweet baby girl with a Hebrew name. She would be bestowed with the name Hannah, which was actually the name of her deceased Jewish grandmother.

While Felice would have no recollection of this ceremony, I wanted her parents to have a positive experience with clergy planning for the baby naming. Having a baby often brings people closer to their religion; they are participating in a miracle of life and see where they fit in the chain of their family's traditional values. Synagogues also have wonderful programming around babies and children. I colead Tot-*Shabbat* for years at Congregation Habonim, a conservative synagogue on the Upper West Side. Parents would come for about ninety minutes to participate in an age-appropriate prayer service. Everyone would hear a bible story and have some challah bread and grape juice before the kids would all go to the bima for a closing prayer, thereby instilling synagogue life in all of these children from a young age. But somewhere long ago, Carrie had de-shuled. She was disappointed with the judgmental Jewish scene she had experienced in New York City. Statistically, it is no surprise that she made a home with a non-Jewish partner who was kind, loving, and supportive of her Jewish identity. Remember, non-Orthodox jews "marry out" at seventy-two percent frequency.[62] Carrie really only prioritized observance of traditions at home and family gatherings that featured Jewish foods.

It goes without saying, the care with which we welcome multiethnic children into the Jewish community should be treated with extra sensitivity. Historically, the narrative of the typical American Jew having roots in Eastern Europe has long been the focus. However, there are Jews of all different races and backgrounds. I grew up with two Black Jews in my small class at Jewish private school. One was a Jewish boy from an Ethiopian refugee family,

---

62   Pew Research Center, "Jewish Americans in 2020," 39.

and another was from a biracial and interfaith marriage whose African American mother had converted to Judaism. I cannot recall any tiptoeing around these classmates and their inclusivity. They were both celebrated members of the class; the Ethiopian boy was a reminder that the Jewish tribes were scattered all around the Middle East and Africa and of the commitment various Jewish agencies had to rescuing Jews in problematic areas of the world. (There were also many refugees from the Former Soviet Union, including one of my best friends, Svetlana.) When that boy's Ethiopian parents visited school, they always dressed a little differently, but they were welcomed with open arms. This boy was one of the more popular kids in the grade and our lockers were almost always next to each other because our last names started with an "E." The African American girl's identity must have been more complex for her; she was born to a white and non-Jewish father and a Black Jewish mother. Her older sister was light-skinned and she was not. I know she felt different from all of the other girls, and not just because she was so much taller. She talked about how we didn't understand her issues with her hair even when we were young. Later in life, I had many North-African or Persian Jewish friends. My closest collaborator, Daniella Rabbani, has a mixed ethnic background with grandparents from both Iran and Europe (who survived the Holocaust). I have encouraged her to write her own memoir. The music director I rely on for my services, Jerome Korman, married an extraordinary Filipino dancer who converted and then became a Conservative rabbi who I mentioned previously in Confession IV. Rabbi Mira Rivera is a deep and wonderful rabbi. She's the world's first Filipino rabbi, breaking ground in her work of outreach to Jews of color (JOCs) and liberal communities. Jerry and Rabbi Mira also have two children of color who are active and expressive in their Jewish indentities. Their daughter, Arielle, is finishing rabbinical training at the Jewish Theological Seminary and cofounded Ammud, The Jews of Color Torah Academy. I have worked with Jerry and Arielle for more than a decade.

While the overwhelming majority of leaders are still white Jews, the Jewish world is aware of its shifting demographics and needs to work better with the diversity in our population. According to the 2020 Pew Research study "Race, ethnicity, heritage, and immigration among US Jews . . . Using the broadest definition of diversity, nearly three-in-ten Jewish adults under thirty (twenty-eight percent) identify as Hispanic, Black, Asian, other race, or multiracial; identify as Sephardic and/or Mizrahi; or are immigrants or children of immigrants to the US from outside Canada, Europe, or the former Soviet Union—compared with a total of seven percent of Jews ages sixty-five and older who meet any of those overlapping dimensions of diversity."[63] The data suggests that interracial marriages within the last forty years, adoption, and immigration can all contribute to the rise in young adults seeing themselves as non-White. This number would include people like my friend, Leon Setton, an excellent licensed clinical social worker with whom I went to New York University. When we first met at NYU, I was so happy to meet another Jew from an observant background, as he went to the Yeshivah of Flatbush in Brooklyn. However, my obsession with the Yiddish language and theater was lost on him. His identity was deeply linked to being Egyptian and how his family was expelled from the Arab country due to antisemitism and Israel's founding. He would later participate in many "JOCs" forums and teach me the phrase "Ashkinormative," meaning the perceived norm of Jewish culture is the Ashkenazi experience. We must do better to weave the stories and customs of JOCs into the fabric of what it means to be Jewish. There are some great organizations out there dealing with racial diversity

---

63   Ibid, 175.

in Judaism, including Jews in ALL Hues and the Jews of Color Initiative. Still, as a European Jew, I'm not offered spots in these workshops and my sensitivity training is limited to my own life experience, reading, practice, and barometer of fairness.

I understood how important it was to welcome Felice and her parents into this Jewish naming ritual and set the tone for the rest of her life of positive Jewish participation. I also knew how important it would be to engage Don in the process. Any moment with his daughter would be emotional—and we were going to celebrate her background and nod to many parts of her identity. I reasoned that if Don felt included now then he would continue to feel included in the rest of her Jewish upbringing. For me the stakes were high: this was the only way Felice would have a shot at having any other Jewish milestones in her life. I asked Don way more questions than I did Carrie. I heard about how he came to the states to play professional sports, worked in real estate, and had an older daughter as well as lots of extended family who would be present and participating in the baby naming. Don told me he always wanted a Hebrew name and I told him his name was already Hebrew! Dan, one of the twelve sons of Jacob became one of the twelve tribes of Israel. He loved that a part of him was already Jewish. Don named his oldest daughter Destiny as he had a lot of feelings about how to let a child's destiny unfold. Not yet a parent, I listened to the teachings he could share with me.

The makeup of this modern family would be different than just parents, siblings, grandparents, and cousins. Carrie's parents had both passed away. There were no Jewish grandparents to visit in Florida who make delicious brisket and hamantaschen cookies. Carrie had no siblings and therefore Felice would have no Jewish cousin table at holiday gatherings. Carrie had selected godparents, who were friends with her own parents, to be part of Felice's life. You can tell even from the term "godparent," that the custom is taken from the Christian world, and maybe even from Carrie's Italian Catholic side. Don had a very involved brother who would serve as an uncle. Don's daughter Destiny, was already over eighteen years old, and lived in a different state. Her involvement in Felice's life was still taking shape. The naming ceremony would take place in one of Don's cousin's restaurants, a Latin-Caribbean restaurant in Prospect Park, Brooklyn.

In one of my meetings with Don and Carrie, we went through the entire ceremony, assigning roles for each section. I mentioned where there were moments to add flourishes or to incorporate aspects of Don's Dominican roots and he said that it would be covered with the food and in all the participants there. He was excited to do something authentically Jewish, that was not diluted by other influences. The form of my *Simchat bat* ceremony has six main components:

1. A welcome with a song and a few short words about the ceremony's format. I usually tie in the week's proper portion of the Torah to give a nod to the tradition of naming a baby during the Torah reading.
2. A blessing is made over the mother for having survived the dangers of childbearing.
3. Readings are shared by the family members present. I like to involve the family by asking them to read various English readings, like poems, especially about Jewish women. These readings sometimes change depending on the family's needs.
4. A short speech is delivered by the parents, either separate or together.
5. I bless the child with a traditional prayer in Hebrew and bestow upon them a Hebrew name that also incorporates the names of their parents.

6. We close out the service with a meaningful song, either from the Jewish canon or pop culture.

I mentioned to Carrie and Don there could be one more area to add a special touch. In Jewish culture, often superstition dictates religious practice. The evil eye is a symbol in many Middle Eastern cultures and Jewish people do plenty of things to ward it off, like spitting or saying "no evil eye" or "*kein ayin hara*" in the presence of something positive. More superstitious Jews don't post pictures of their families and children to tempt the evil eye. Even when lighting Friday night candles, some Sephardic Jews have the custom of waving their hands in an outward motion before covering their eyes to cast out any evil energy. There happens to be a similar ceremony to a baby naming known as a *Pidyon Haben*, a redemption of the oldest male child, so long as both parents are not descendants from the Levite tribe or priestly Cohen family. During the ceremony, the baby boy is redeemed from the priest by offering five silver coins. While this service is really only done in Orthodox circles, one of the customs I particularly like is that the baby is surrounded by sugar cubes and garlic as a good omen; sugar for a sweet life and garlic for plentiful blessings and fulfillment of commandments. For many of my baby naming clients, I encourage them to come up with a sweet item with which to surround their child.

Don replied instantly, "Oh I know exactly what we'll do. We were already planning on giving out black and white cookies because that's what we are: a black and white cookie. It's the quintessential New York dessert and it's who we are and who Felice is: black and white." I laughed and was relieved. This savvy couple understood the assignment and knocked it out the park. They were finding a way to make it work in the context of their tradition, sensitivity, *and* sense of humor. The iconic *New*

York Times food columnist Melissa Clark, wrote once: "Black-and-whites have been an entrenched part of the very robust Jewish cookie scene in New York City for a century."[64] I felt like everything was coming together—no wonder some people call it the "unity cookie." I renamed the event in my calendar "Black and White Cookie Naming." I couldn't wait to officiate for them.

About a week after this conversation, my partner, Ben, asked me to go to Australia to meet his gravely ill stepfather before he passed away from cancer. I was stuck between a rock and a hard place. As a rabbi, I have a duty to the families I serve, events I help plan, and communities I build. However, I had longed to find a partner like Ben. I knew that this trip wasn't a vacation; this was my only chance to meet a dying member of his family, to support him and his mother, and to start our lives together. A trip to Australia, without any plane delays, is about a day in transit, and I'd have to give up a week of work. I have almost every weekend booked more than a year in advance with weddings and bar mitzvahs that I am leading. There was only one week that I could travel, and it meant I would have to miss Felice's baby naming.

I had done a considerable amount of work already and had fallen in love with this couple and their family story. I had not been paid a cent for my work, but I felt entirely responsible for finding them a substitute if I were to cancel on them. If I worked for an institution, I'd be entitled to a life, sick days, and personal days. But I am not just a rabbi, I run my own teaching practice. I work for myself and have to rely on my network of friends and colleagues to cover for me if something comes up. Most times I have had no luck partnering with other clergy who are tied to an organization because their organization limits their abilities to

---

64 Clark, Melissa. n.d. "Black-and-White Cookies." *Tablet Magazine.* https://100jewishfoods.tabletmag.com/black-and-white-cookies/.

serve non-members. My challenge is to find like-minded, similarly practicing Jewish professionals who are dedicated, available, and qualified to step in for me. There are many liberal rabbis out there who are okay with facilitating interfaith family life cycle moments, but there are only a select few that are a spiritual match to me. If someone has come to me, they are seeking someone mainstream, modern, traditional, inspiring, authentic, worldly, with-it, and open minded. That is harder to find than you think. I have found it in just a few partners, and one of my favorites to collaborate with is Rabbi Rachel Rosenbluth who often goes by Bluth.

I heard of Bluth a few months before I met her. A great friend from the world of theater producing, Caitlin Fitzwater, started participating in a program that Bluth cofounded. An online monthly subscription program for the loosely affiliated or Jewishly curious, School of Living Jewishly (SOLJ), had members from all over the world learning about the weekly Torah portion and holidays with podcasts, live learning sessions, and question forums. Caitlin kept telling me what a great experience she was having with the program and encouraged me to become a member. I joined and started their Shabbat session guide. I enjoyed Bluth's soothing voice and the artistic learning guides. When my best friend in Tel Aviv, Aaron Gelbman, mentioned the program too, I doubled down and joined their book club. They were reading *Here All Along* by Sarah Hurwitz. The book explains how and why the former speechwriter for Michelle Obama came to rediscover her deep connection to Judaism. I enjoyed the book and the online gathering, especially during the pandemic. Offline, one of SOLJ's facilitators asked me who I was and if I wanted to get more involved in the program and I expressed interest in meeting Bluth. Soon, we met for a long afternoon when she was visiting New York from Canada, and I instantly felt a connection.

If I'm the "glamor rabbi" she's the "bohemian rabbi." Bluth

grew up similarly to myself, and moved to Israel. As a mixed medium visual artist and Jewish facilitator, she was drawn to a unique Israeli rabbinical seminary, Beit Midrash Har'el, that provides *semicha*, ordination, to women and men. Bluth has a worldly sense about her, having spent time almost everywhere: India, Africa, and the US. She has zero ego and doesn't enjoy leading ceremonies as much as she enjoys training others to become leaders. I could tell that she was open to partnership from the second we met over iced coffees in Brooklyn. She told me about ideas for a television show, more work within SOLJ, and her ever expanding artistic portfolio. I knew one day I'd ask her to be my artist for my *ketubah* (marriage contract).

For Carrie and Don, I reached out to Bluth. I thought she would be the right person to handle this life cycle moment for them. I figured Bluth would be into the Dominican Republic-New York fusion, Black and White Cookie Baby Naming. She was, and I was so grateful. I passed all my notes to her, my draft service, and she took it from there. Bluth ushered baby Felice into her first blessings as a Jewish woman. It was bittersweet that I didn't get to the finish line with Felice, but in some ways, it was even sweeter to pass the work and opportunity to my colleague and friend. The experience helped Bluth and I build trust and a sort of partnership. I continued my journey around the world to Australia to meet Ben's stepfather of nearly twenty years.

When people asked me how I found Australia, I joked that I didn't realize how almost everyone there spoke Russian. Most of my time in Australia was spent around Ben's family, half of which came from Belarus as refugees escaping antisemitism in the late 1970s. The other half of his family is Polish and survived the Holocaust. Everyone in Ben's generation had a combination of an Eastern European accent mixed with the gorgeous Aussie tone. But Ben's mother, Sonia, and his stepfather spoke to each other almost exclusively in Russian. The heavy sound of the Russian language added to the palpable sadness around the illness and time in their lives.

At over six foot three, Tolik was an enormous presence even fifty pounds lighter after cancer treatments. Tolik was at times jovial and others extremely austere. Only seventy-five years old and with less than a year since his diagnosis, he was aware that he was dying, and soon. He chain smoked on the outdoor porch and sat with the endless visitors who wanted to experience his sharp wit for as long as they could. Ben's devoted sisters, Natalie and Lisa, were always by their mother's side. Sonia managed Tolik's medicine, kept house, and fed endless amounts of guests during the drawn-out illness and decline. I wanted to do my best to support Ben and his family and get a sense of Tolik in his final days. For me, the strong plumes of cigarette smoke were hard to bear. Besides having osmophobia, a sensitivity to strong smells, (and them triggering my migraines), I was upset that we were all inhaling dangerous smoke that very well could have led to his cancer in the first place. I've never touched or smoked a cigarette in my life. I have always hated them and have known the risk they pose to people's health. I was caught between my personal feelings against these cancer sticks and feeling sympathetic towards a dying man and the culture of enjoying a cigarette. Still, I was happy to spend some time with him. I saw his eyes twinkle when he saw his grandchildren, talked about how he built himself from nothing, and expressed loyalty to Jewish people around the world. Ben was comforted by my support and I knew I made the choice of missing work to invest deeper in my personal relationship. On our trip back from Australia, Ben and I discussed getting engaged in the near future.

Tolik passed away in August of 2023. The same day of his passing, strangely, I got an email from Carrie asking me or Rabbi Bluth the following request:

"Hi Rabbis! Hope you're both well! Our family friend is getting married in April 2024 in Kennebunkport, Maine and Felice is the flower girl! They are doing a nondenominational ceremony but would like a rabbi to do a small ketubah signing service on Friday night before the wedding (April 19, 2024). So, we are looking for a rabbi who wouldn't already be doing Shabbat services at their congregation and it's also the weekend before Passover. Do either of you know anyone in that area who might be a fit or able to do this? The groom is Jewish and the bride is not and neither are religious. Thank you both in advance."

I can't express how disappointing this message was to me. On the one hand, I really wanted to continue to serve this family, but I felt like their request was completely tone-deaf. They were asking for the impossible. Did we know a rabbi in Maine, (total Jewish Population a mere 12,550)[65] who wouldn't already be serving their own community on a Friday night, and one who would be willing to perform an interfaith wedding (not permitted) on the Sabbath (weddings are not permitted on the Sabbath) *before* Passover? All of those requests alone would be hard, but together they sounded like she really didn't understand what she was asking. Perhaps mixed with my grief over Tolik's death, I couldn't handle the absurdity of the request. *Why would the couple even need a ketubah if they weren't having a Jewish wedding or a Jewish marriage?* I got hung up on the legality: having an intermarriage and holding the signing ceremony on the Sabbath would render the ketubah not kosher anyways. To me it was the equivalent of asking us to celebrate Hanukkah in July and in outer space. I told her that it was highly unlikely she would find a rabbi who would

---

65 "Jewish Population by State 2024." n.d. 2024 World Population Review. Accessed 2024. https://worldpopulationreview.com/state-rankings/jewish-population-by-state.

be available and willing to plan this event for her loved ones. If it was important to them to have such a ceremony they should work within the framework of the Jewish Calendar. I also sent her a basic national list of rabbis she could check, but as Bluth and I are flexible as they come, I thought it was unlikely.

The whole exchange left me feeling uncomfortable and unsure. As someone who safeguards Judaism, even for modern people in a flexible way, I felt a boundary violation. It was really important for me to stand my ground and center myself. I don't have to serve everyone and fulfill every request to keep people engaged and Jewish. I can always fill my hours with meaningful work, and don't have to give up my integrity. I'm constantly sacrificing my personal life and time, unsure of whether or not I feel good about bending my life into a pretzel. This last request was the last straw. I was actually offended by the insensitivity to Jewish customs and basic framework around a Jewish wedding. I would not have anything to do with this wedding. As a protector of our religion, did not even pass the request on to another provider. This is the end of my relationship with Carrie, Don, and Felice.

Below is a section from the custom readings assembled for Felice's baby naming. They are readings selected by myself and by Rabbi Rosenbluth adapted from various religious texts:

My daughter, do not forget the Torah; let your mind retain the Mitzvot. May they bestow upon you length of days, years of life, and well-being. Let love and truth never leave you; wear them as a necklace, write them upon the tablet of your heart, and may you find grace and good favor in the eyes of G-d and humanity. (Proverbs 3:1–4)

Brucha haba'ah b'shem Adonay. Brucha at ba'ir, ubrucha at basadeh. Welcome to the one who arrives in the name of all things

Holy. Blessed are you in the cities and in nature. (Psalm 118:26,
Translation adapted by Rabbi Rebecca Keren Jablonski)

Brucha at b'voekha, ubrucha at b'tzetekh. Welcome little one!
Blessed may you be all your days, all your life; blessed may you be
wherever you are, In all of your comings and in all of your goings.
(Deuteronomy 28:3,[66] *Adapted by Rabbi Rachel Rosenbluth)*

There is a new light in our hearts and in our family. We celebrate
the birth of a new child. We celebrate her emergence into light.
Child of light, we greet you with love and joy overflowing from
our hearts. (Text by Rabbi Rachel Rosenbluth)

In the end, it is a difficult task to thread the needle of adapting
our religion to modern people's family makeups. Carrie and Don
were not the first interfaith family I worked with by a long shot,
and they won't be the last. It was through sensitive collabora-
tion with them and another like-minded independent rabbi that
we were able to provide them with a religious experience. At the
same time, what kind of rabbi would I be if I had zero limits or
boundaries? Saying no is just as important as saying yes—in fact
there are 365 commandments phrased in the negative, 117 more
than the 248 phrased in the positive. Setting my own limits as a
Jewish professional is important; that I only have to answer to
my own religious and moral compasses is the benefit of working
the way I do. While we are on the subject: I am not simply a
"rent-a-rabbi," and find that term offensive. Just because I may
not be part of one religious denomination or another, I've found
the ability within myself to say what feels right or wrong, and

---

66   The Jewish Publication Society. 1985. JPS TANAKH: *The Holy Scriptures*
     (Blue): The New JPS Translation According to the Traditional Hebrew Text.
     The Jewish Publication Society.

stick with it. I wish everyone the fortitude to turn down work when asked to do something with which they are uncomfortable. More than that, I am glad I chose to invest in my personal life. To every entrepreneur out there, to every social servant out there: life can be greater than just a career and financial success. I had long given up dates, social engagements, friends' weddings, and more to build my client list. When Ben and I started a relationship, I knew deep down that I had to reorganize my priorities. I was right and I'm so grateful I listened to my gut. For me, building a family is another way of fulfilling my dreams, investing in the future of the Jewish people, and filling my heart. Be brave to say no to some things and it will make room for others in your life. Now, Ben and I hang our ketubah in our home, masterfully designed and executed by Bluth.

CONFESSION IX:
I love huge, over the top, parties.

"This is my God and I will glorify Him"
—EXODUS 15:2

Case Study 6

I was an acquaintance of the Pro Football Hall of Fame, New York Giants defensive back, Michael Strahan, for a few years. He is currently an American television icon: cohost of ABC's *Good Morning America*, analyst for *Fox NFL Sunday*, a fashion mogul, game show host, and more. Before all that, I used to live in the same building as him on the Upper West Side, walking distance from ABC studios. The same summer that Michael got the gig replacing Regis Philbin as Kelly Ripa's cohost of a morning talk show, my sister, who was also my roommate, got married. And like married people do, my sister moved out of our apartment. That left me with an extra bedroom. Michael had an incredible female trainer who was commuting back and forth from New Jersey and Los Angeles. She needed to live in the building if he was going to meet his fitness goals and trim down for TV. Our mutual housekeeper and the doorman let him know I was looking to sublet my sister's furnished bedroom. The *shidduch,* match, was made.

Training a football hero was enough of a reference for me. The first night that she came to meet me she was so stunning, fit, and full of energy. I was exhausted—I had just taught an entire day. I stopped her midsentence when she was thinking where she'd put her Vitamix blender and protein supplements. My only requirement was that she kept *kosher*, Jewish dietary laws. Perhaps this was a challenging set of rules to explain to a Catholic, African American woman who was more than ten years my senior. But she was a vegan, so we were a great pair. We agreed that if she cooked for Michael, she would buy meat at the local kosher butcher or from FreshDirect's kosher supply. Yes, he and others ate kosher if it came from our kitchen.

I lived with Latreal Mitchell for three awesome years. A former body builder from the Bronx, "La" found her calling in fitness training. She was a completely self-made and an independent woman. I still got some financial help from my parents, and they were the guarantors of this apartment. Latreal was physically stronger than most men. She didn't need a man to be happy and was able to walk away from bad relationships. She was gorgeous, smart, and an inspiring small business owner. She pushed me to grow up. She was my new protector and older sister.

At the time I worked two full time jobs, in Broadway marketing by day and Hebrew and bar mitzvah tutoring by night and on weekends. I still worked holiday or odd shifts at SoulCycle. My parents and mentor, Liz, encouraged me to go to either cantorial or rabbinical school, but I was still stuck between two worlds. However, I was never *just* a teacher. I was everyone's older best friend, making it cool to study and learn about tradition and religion. I grew a waitlist for popular tutoring hours. I went to my students' dance and school performances. I performed as a cantor at ceremony services outside of traditional synagogues. I had started frequently flying to Israel as clients held services by the egalitarian prayer area at the Davidson Center/Robinson's Arch. Sometimes patrons and donors with connections to the Israel Museum in Jerusalem used one of the replica synagogues that operated mostly as an exhibit as the location for their service. Occasionally, I got a role as an actress in a show and somehow balanced it all. Latreal cooked and trained for Strahan and managed several clients. We were both single and worked our butts off.

With Latreal's introduction, she and I began working for the same family (Latreal as a trainer and myself as a Hebrew tutor). The Rabin family was also friends with Michael Strahan. They both had connections to sports, fashion, Senator Cory Booker, and others. I was about to work with the family all on my own when I realized they had previously been a client with a tutoring company with which I contracted for years. I never wanted to take business away from this company. Door to Door Tutoring and Joel Cohen gave me a start in New York City, and provided me with great work experience. I emailed the business administrator and Joel to let them know that the prior tutor was being let go and would be replaced by me. I put all my work with the family through the tutoring company, and they took a large commission. Once I became a rabbi, it was no longer wise for me to work within his company for my regular teaching and facilitation.

So back to the family who is the focus of this case study. The middle child was scheduled to celebrate becoming a bar mitzvah on February 20, 2016. The bar mitzvah was a late Saturday afternoon service with a party to follow.

The Venue: The Barclays Center stadium in Brooklyn.

The Attire: Black and White.

The Expectations: HUGE.

For years I taught Brandon and his two other siblings. Our lessons consisted of Jewish holidays, Hebrew reading, prayers, and finally a special Torah portion for his service. He worked as hard as he could to prepare. The best part of our studying always came when we would cuddle with one of his three dogs, cook something holiday-related with his siblings, act silly together, or have a heart-to-heart. This boy was a little shy and had a heart of gold. He got it from his mother, Nicole. Some see her as stand-offish but she is extremely kind, welcoming, and playful. She lost her sister, Charna, at a young age to illness. Her family was her life. I felt so blessed to be in her orbit. Giving back in her sister's memory was also very important. That became the focus of Brandon's charity project associated with his bar mitzvah.

It is a mitzvah for every Jew to participate in creating a Torah scroll. Brandon's family decided to commission a new and gorgeous Torah scroll dedicated to the memory of family members who had passed away. For years, Joel and I would rent Torah scrolls and would dream of having our own company Torah to make everything easier and more accessible for our services outside of synagogue walls. I told Joel that I thought the Rabins would be interested in partnering to commission a Torah Scroll. The concept of *hiddur mitzvah*, beautifying a command to elevate one's own observance, was not lost on this elegant and stylish family. For several months, the family, Joel, and I sat with a scribe as he explained all the rules for writing the family's sacred Torah. The Torah would have custom sterling silver engraving on its wooden poles, an ornate dress, and a silver decorative breastplate and crown. Joel would keep it for future use at services with Door-to-Door Tutoring families. The month before this Brooklyn bar mitzvah, the family traveled to Israel to do a service in Jerusalem and pick up their commissioned Torah. I already had a conflict; a bat mitzvah at Central Synagogue with a private tutoring client— interestingly linked to the landlords of the apartment building where I met everyone in the first place. I was planning to leave right after sundown on Saturday. However, the Northeast was slammed with a record blizzard named Jonas, and my flight was canceled. The whole weekend was chaotic. I tried to rebook a flight but it was no use. I missed the whole Israel celebration. I was so disappointed that I wasn't in the Holy Land celebrating this boy's studies and his family's deep commitment to all things Jewish. I wanted to be a part of the first use of this Torah. But it is humbling to remember, no person can out-plan G-d or the weather.

It fascinated me that a family so invested in Jewish life was not seeking to work within the confines of a synagogue institution. While the family had tried various Hebrew school options, they didn't stick. Synagogue structure couldn't meet this extraordinary family's needs. This family moved to Hong Kong for a year to accommodate the father's work. They had a relationship with a Chabad rabbi. But at the same time, the family came from the Conservative movement. And, they didn't enjoy the modern musical changes they noticed at many of the Manhattan synagogues and longed for something traditional. The family didn't observe strict Jewish law (other than during Passover) and therefore never felt like the many traditional synagogue offerings in New York felt like home. They had many children with different schedules. They lead extraordinary lives. They decided to build their own community with friends and family and leaned on Joel, other Jewish professionals, and myself to create it in a meaningful way. Their Torah without an ark, traveling from lifecycle moment to moment, was a symbol for their dedication to these ideals.

In the final days leading up to his Brooklyn service, I realized how huge this event was becoming. We would have team planning meetings with the legendary event planner Michael Cerbelli, Gourmet Advisory Services, and our orchestra and music directors. It *seemed* totally extra. Yet, it didn't matter to me if we were doing a backyard or a stadium bar mitzvah—maybe that's because I come from a performance background and I'm just used to singing in huge halls. I love big productions. I'll be really honest: every synagogue service outside of the Orthodox movement has a lot of performance elements. The family had stylists dropping off racks of clothes. Boxes lined their halls with outfits and religious artifacts that they would use for the service. Brandon had secret rehearsals at the Barclays for his entrance. He would fly in from the rafters of the stadium on a wire with pyrotechnics and fog shooting up on either side of him. *Obviously!* For the service, we rehearsed several times in sound studios with a band of more than twenty talented musicians, and even two professional cantors. We recorded tracks of our songs to prepare Max Weinberg of the E Street Band/Tonight Show Band who would be drumming in the service. It is true, I had never been part of such a *huge* production for a coming-of-age ceremony. I didn't even know how big it would be until I was there.

Sometimes I worried that the Jewish values behind a bar mitzvah were being lost. I reminded the party planner, no matter what, I needed to be next to the boy at all times during the service to keep him queued, focused, and calm. I got frustrated at the hype of the party planning and how it ate into my study time. Furthermore, I was overextended in my own schedule and under-caffeinated. In the final months before Brandon's celebration, one of my other students had deliberately placed a Torah scroll on the floor. I wasn't even there—he FaceTime video chatted me with the rented and unfurled Torah scroll. He had placed it on the floor in order to locate his Torah portion and practice. This is considered to be a grave offense to the holy artifact. Dropping a Torah bears a communal fasting punishment for any adults who see the offense. I shrieked at this child over the phone, told him first to pick up the Torah, and second, that I'd be there in ten minutes to help put it away. I frantically sought counsel from friends that were rabbis as to how I should handle the fast. None said that I would have to do a full forty-day fast, as it was through a video screen that I witnessed the Torah on the floor. "Do we fast every time we see a photograph or documentary from the Holocaust and recall how the Nazis destroyed our holy artifacts?" Still, I couldn't handle that no one would take responsibility for dropping the Torah. If someone should take responsibility, it should be me. I should have taught him better. I had decided to fast for forty days, from sunup to sundown. Imagine: working out in the gym, working all day, and then tutoring at night, fasting for forty days, and trying to have patience with kids. I'd break my fast with a protein bar and water after sundown and then pig out late nights after teaching. The forty days went on longer than you think, because we do not fast on Saturdays and Hanukkah, so what was counted as forty days, actually stretched into a fifty-five-day ordeal. So many of my students saw firsthand how seriously I took respect for the Torah scroll and I'm glad that I shared my fasting experience.

Even though I felt pressure to get Brandon ready for this big day, I believed his parents had their hearts in the right place. I remember all the discussions we had about Jewish life and the importance of our traditions. I sat many times with both sets of doting grandparents and learned about their family histories. I remembered the family's deep commitment to charity, the Jewish faith, and their Torah scroll. Their children were as sweet as sugar. All three were a little shy and loved animals. I did my best to keep the bar mitzvah about the service. The parents had the means and the connections to throw an epic party for their son and community, so it wasn't my place to tell them how to celebrate. They were building an experience to hold the grandeur of the event: their son becoming a Jewish adult. To them, this was a huge spiritual moment. The synagogues in our city couldn't contain their vision. Only the Barclays Center was big enough.

Back to the bar mitzvah. The service was in the atrium in the Calvin Klein VIP entrance of the Barclays Center. It was a beautifully transformed hall with a platform, podium, and custom-built holy ark. The separate chamber housed the band playing pop songs, led by Jerome Korman, and a graffiti portrait of the thirteen-year-old boy, juxtaposing Brooklyn and Jerusalem in the background.

Right before we were about to start the service, in walked Michael Strahan with his girlfriend and driver. Michael gave me a huge hug. He was kind, and laughed at how our worlds collided. As he took his seat, I joined the family. We were standing in the back of the hall waiting to make our grand entrance. First, a film was shown to explain the creation of a Torah. I was annoyed, because whoever worked on the film had used Hebrew letters, but they were all backwards and wrong. I believe in being impeccable with details and felt like a protector over the legitimacy of the whole event—even though we were in a basketball stadium. Suddenly, two horn blowers sounded the ancient ram's horn, the *shofar*. Then Max Weinberg, with a strap-on snare drum, set a beat and marched down the center aisle of the room. Max joined his large band and they played a rock and roll horah medley. The family of grandparents, parents, siblings, and cousins marched down the center aisle. The bar mitzvah boy, under a chuppah canopy supported by his grandparents, was holding his Torah like a precious baby. While totally over the top, this is Jewish tradition—every new Torah scroll is like receiving the first Torah scroll. Communities make large parties to march in a new Torah for its first official use with tremendous fanfare. I danced with the group at the front of the stage, and there was nothing but joy and love in the room. When the song was over, the family and orchestra took their seats. Joel and I began the service with Brandon.

Brandon must have been petrified—five hundred of his closest family and friends watching him. There was also live video feed and screens all over so the people in the back could see what was happening on the bima. It was like a religious sporting event. Every family member had a part in the service. There was a guest male cantor from a Brooklyn synagogue and a guest female facilitator with a guitar. They each had one "prayer solo" song. I would cue any songs that the bar mitzvah boy would do as a solo—sometimes with a look, or whisper in his ear, or a pointer on the page. He did a great job on every part. His siblings and family did too. Then it came time for me to give him a speech and a blessing. I hugged him and cried. I told him how sweet and thoughtful he is as a person. I reminded him what a tremendous family he comes from and what an honor it is to be his teacher. His mother gave a touching speech and was kind enough to thank me, calling me one of her family, and my tears kept coming. The service was a huge success and set the tone for why the family was throwing this enormous celebration.

The party was so crazy I can't possibly remember every detail. There was drum-drill-band flanking every aisle as the guests walked through the stadium from one destination to another. The cocktails and appetizers were in the 40/40 Club. Two artists with chainsaws carved a block of ice into a sculpture as a different cover band played classic hits. There was Nobu sushi, Peter Luger steak, and beyond. I keep kosher so I only drink water or tequila-based cocktails at these events. (Yes, by the end of the day, I was starved.) I hung back with Michael Strahan and his friends for a while. I had a very religious boyfriend who kept all the rules of the Jewish Sabbath. He joined the party only once Shabbat was officially over. He was conflicted about seeing these types of modern religious services and seeing me lead prayers in public. In his Haredi community, female rabbis were unheard of, let alone men and women praying together, and about a hundred other things that were unorthodox in this service. While I cared for him, you can see why this wasn't going to work out long-term.

The time came to enter the main stadium for the party and we walked into the gorgeously lit arena with music blasting and more drummers lined on each side. You could see the inside of the stadium had been turned into a carnival, complete with two huge roller coasters, games, and enormous video screens. The R&B legend Aaron Neville sang the mother-son dance "First Time Ever I Saw Your Face." At about 11:30 p.m., Pitbull, "Mr. World-wide," came out with dancers and performed his most popular songs. It was epic and fun. Pitbull made a point of telling Brandon and his crowd how lucky we all were. He shared that he got his start as a wedding and bar mitzvah hype dancer, and here he was performing in one of the largest venues in New York for a bar mitzvah. It was a full circle moment to keep us humble—even if we were living in a fantasy world for just one night. In any event, the family and guests had a killer time. Holy Moses, it was super.

The next morning, I had to teach at eight. With barely any sleep and the previous night's makeup still intact, I got ready to do the real work. I taught for twelve hours straight, no break, just taxis in between students, and continued to coach several other kids for their big days. I received several emails and text messages asking me if I had anything to do with the crazy bar mitzvah in the city last night. People wanted me to tell them about it. I didn't want to partake in the city gossip. I kept a tight Sunday schedule of lessons so I didn't participate much in the buzz.

At about 6 p.m. that Monday, I got a text message from the bar mitzvah boy, Brandon. It was a YouTube link and a message "Go to min. 6:00." I clicked on the link and it was *Live with Kelly and Michael*. Michael Strahan was giving a rundown of his weekend and he talked about the amazing bar mitzvah at the Barclays Center and Pitbull's performance. He left out many of these details and Kelly made a few jokes. But then something really special happened.

Michael mentioned me. Not by name, but by my connection through his trainer, Latreal, and my role. He spent the last full minute of his weekend wrap up talking about what it meant to see the bar mitzvah coach up there with the bar mitzvah boy too. Yes, there was morning talk show fluff in there, but all kidding aside, he brought the meaning back. No one understands the role of the coach more than an athlete. It was nice to be acknowledged, but more meaningful to know that the work I did really stood out. That being a mentor and a support system for these kids was evident. This process of becoming a Jewish adult is hard and rigorous, and so the role of a teacher is huge. I'm not just "the help," or there to prepare the child for thirty minutes of singing. My role included true coaching, character building, man- and woman-making, and religious training. How good of Michael to understand it and mention it. Maybe Max Weinberg was bummed he didn't make the cut when Strahan was summarizing the night. Even the rollercoasters weren't mentioned. But what was mentioned was the teaching. And by the way, Torah means "teaching," which is the whole point of this bar mitzvah: *that's what it was all for.*

It's a complicated thing when someone has an over-the-top party because the competition sets in within the community. Every child wants to have the most fabulous service or party, and their parents want to feel like the biggest *makhers,* big shots. This family wasn't competing—it's not their nature. (Trust me, in 2015, I shared a suite with them in Jerusalem for several days. I know them.) They were sharing the blessings they have: access to the Barclays Center and the disposable income to shower their children and friends with an over-the-top fun night. I hope other children know that their big day will be special, too, and that it is *not* fair to compare. Children are special not because of the material things they have, and the sooner they understand that, the better. It is also important to teach children that someone will always have more than you and someone will always have less; I always say "those who keep score are always the losers." Again, I'll do my part to get their minds right. This city has endless ways to feel in competition or inadequate. I have to strengthen each child from within to be happy with their own portion.

Below is Brandon's speech on his special Torah, donations, and even a little mention of income inequality:

The Torah portion for this Shabbat Mincha Service is called Ki Tisa. It centers around the idea of giving donations to G-d for the building of the Mishkan, which was the Israelites' traveling sanctuary while traveling through Sinai. Interestingly, G-d mentions to Moses that the rich should not give more and the poor should not give a lesser amount of Shekels, or silver donations. (SWALLOW)

My family was inspired to give a donation as well. (SWALLOW)

As you are now aware, about a year ago my family embarked on the journey of creating a Sefer Torah. Working with Joel, my family, and a sofer, a Jewish Scribe in Israel, to create this Torah all showed me how important and special this artifact is for the Jewish people.

A Torah is beautiful—maybe even the most beautiful thing I have ever helped make and if treated properly, a Torah can last longer than anything I will own in mine or anyone else's life.

I made something that is going to last forever, and many people will be able to use it for their special simchas, like bar/bat mitzvahs, baby namings, weddings, and holidays. It will be passed on for many generations to come. Even my grandchildren will get to use this Torah for their bar or bat mitzvah when they step up and become a man or a woman in Judaism! So hard to imagine but true! (SWALLOW)

One of the things that was most exciting about creating the Torah was seeing how it was made. Before the sofer even writes one letter they have to go in the mikveh, the sacred ritual bath, to be clean and purify themselves before the act of writing. They always start their day with writing G-d's name first, because it is then that they are the most awake and focused. The scribe has to follow every single rule and get every single letter right.

The handwriting looks so beautiful, written with special ink and a special quill. The scribe who wrote my Torah spent an entire year writing, day after day. The scribe was dedicating his entire life to the process, and that is all he does. (SWALLOW)

I thought about the scribe. I thought about how much money he must make for a year. A Torah is very valuable, but at the same time, a scribe does not make that much money. Certainly, he does not make nearly as much as someone like, let's say . . . Lebron James!

However, I believe the scribe requires way more focus than Lebron would. They both have to be dedicated, skilled, and perfect at what they do. If Lebron misses a shot people get mad and he does not win. If a scribe makes a mistake, he has to start the entire section over, and lose a full day's work.

But there is a huge difference in how much they are paid. Also, what is interesting is that Lebron is famous, and I am sure there is not even one person in this room who could mention by name a scribe.

This tells me a lot about values: it does not matter who or what made something, sometimes we only care about the product and the end result. When I get a shoe, I think about the brand and the design itself, I do not necessarily think about all of the hands that touched the shoe so that it could be made. I think that this might be a negative quality that some of us share and one that I want to change.

We should pay more attention to who actually makes things for us. And forget about sneakers, because these are things that we eventually outgrow. A Torah is not. (SWALLOW)

The Torah is also something that can continue to give forever. A lot of people can benefit from its teachings. My Mitzvah project, of creating this Torah, will allow other people to use it after making a small contribution to Tzedakah, a charity. Their donations will be deposited into a fund that is allocated to various charities that I decide throughout the years. I think I went to about thirty bar or bat mitzvahs this year. To think that I could raise thousands of dollars a year for various charities through my Torah is amazing, and to know that each special occasion that it is used for will add another special element of tzedakah.

Brandon's largest takeaway from the bar mitzvah experience was about his ability to affect future Jewish experience by bringing a Torah into the world. The family chose to donate the Torah to Joel Cohen and Joel uses this Torah weekly to officiate bar and bat mitzvah ceremonies. The Torah goes to people's houses and meets the needs of the Jewish families that weren't being met in their synagogues. Brandon's family's tremendous gift allows hundreds of families to have access to the holiest of Jewish artifacts even though the synagogue route didn't seem appealing. For the Rabin family, they continue to be friends and I watch their children grow in Facebook and Instagram posts. They are all in college or beyond now. They have grown up like their mother; they speak only when they have something important to share, they are loyal friends, and tight with their family. It could be rare that these huge parties always have meaningful, thoughtful, Jewish values behind them, but in most cases I've found that they do. Jewish people understand the need for celebration, sharing, providing for brides and grooms, and enjoying the good times. So often we have pain and suffering befall our personal lives or our people. To make a big deal out of a bar mitzvah or a wedding is a grand expression of *hiddur mtzvah*. Likewise, huge celebrations of life glorify the source of all life— G-d. It's time we stop judging people for the way they decide to spend their money. My economist father would say they are doing great by stimulating the economy, anyways. But if Jewish providers do their jobs right, then huge parties or small backyard celebrations, should all be for the same reasons.

CONFESSION X
I have officiated interfaith marriages,
but never *intentionally*.

Case study 7

On a snowy Saturday night in March of 2021, I met Harrison and Miranda. It was the one-hundred-year anniversary of the first-ever bat mitzvah, and we were gathered to pray and celebrate Harrison's first cousin, Olivia, becoming a bat mitzvah. Olivia's mother was one of seven siblings, and the intimate Shabbat afternoon, evening, and *Havdalah* ceremony was being held at their family's historic farm estate in Upstate New York. *Havdalah* literally means separation; but in this case it is the final prayer that separates out the holiness of the Sabbath and ushers in a new mundane week. We do so with wine, sweet spices like cloves, a braided candle with multiple wicks, and a beautiful melody. Given that we were still enduring the pandemic, Olivia's parents wanted to have only their family and ten of Olivia's friends present. The palatial 460-acre property had even been used to shoot the CW series *Gossip Girl*—so sixty people still felt small. Past Otisville Correctional Facility, horse farms, and winding roads, it was in another world in Dutchess County. The family driver transported me, along with several tweens, in the snowy weather. The stretch Cadillac Escalade was packed with Taylor Swift tunes, iPhone chargers, Dior lip gloss, and my Torah scroll in the trunk.

When I got to the sprawling home, I greeted one of my favorite music directors and colleagues, David Hertzberg, who was warming up physically and musically. He had arrived earlier and was dealing with microphones and guitar plugins. The family's spacious living room was transformed into our elegant synagogue. I had to rehearse Olivia with the microphone and Torah, making sure she was comfortable in the space. I competed with the event photographer who wanted to shoot angelic pictures of her in the snow. After a two hour drive, with just thirty minutes of set up and prep, other family guests started to arrive. The noise and stress started to get to me. I escaped to the bathroom, changed into a glamorous pink dress, and put on some makeup.

Right before I was ready to start the ceremony, Harrison and Miranda were presented by Olivia's aunt and uncle. Leslye and Andrew had been married for thirty-three years and had made their idyllic home in Scarsdale, an upper-middle-class town in West Chester, NY. They raised three boys, all in serious relationships.

"Rabbi Becky! We want you to meet Harrison and Miranda. They just got engaged! They have been together for a while but Miranda isn't Jewish!"

It was no question that this couple was deeply in love with each other; both Miranda and Harrison lead with open hearts and kindness in their gaze. Miranda's big wide eyes also told me she was hungry or thirsty, curious to learn more, interested in her partner's religion, and longing for something even within herself.

I gave Miranda a big hug to welcome her. We chatted a little but the noise and my duties for the impending service were first on my mind. She was from Wisconsin and never before attended a bar or bat mitzvah. This was the last little social exchange before Olivia's mother tapped me on the shoulder and told me she wanted to start the service. We began to pray and I couldn't shake my short conversation with Miranda and Harrison from my mind. I made it a point to introduce every prayer or moment in the service as if I were explaining to someone who would be interested in one day making this her own life. I'm not sure anyone noticed how I changed the way I typically led a service, as few of the guests had been to one of my ceremonies anyways. Each rabbi has different ways of introducing prayers. Instinctually, I understood that Miranda was a sponge and if presented in the right way, she would soak up this experience. *Was the subtext of that warm introduction by Harrison's parents to interest Miranda in converting?* Jews do not actively proselytize, and so this was as far out on a limb as I was comfortable going.

The service was beautiful. Olivia was beaming from her accomplishment. Truly, Olivia could have had almost any teacher and done a phenomenal job at her portion and prayers. But Olivia was such a perfectionist, part of my work with her was to loosen her up. She was one of those girls who would say "sorry" all the time. She'd stress over a grade of ninety-eight percent on a school test because she missed a perfect score by two points. I wanted to bring her into adulthood knowing there would be many mistakes or errors along the way, but how we cover or recover is equally important. I didn't want her to apologize unless she did something to hurt another person. That mistakes are part of every process I hope was a takeaway from our studies. I think I got through to her during our sessions. Regardless, everyone was just so proud and happy.

During the night, I really bonded with the troves of cousins, most of whom were in my age group. Due to the weather, I could not get a car service to take me back to Manhattan. While I was worried about my dog (who was being watched by one of my other students back in the city), I had fun dancing, drinking, and singing with the live cover band playing in their grandparent's elegant living room. The patriarch of the family, well into his eighties, grabbed my hand several times and kissed it with gratitude for all I had done for his granddaughter. The cousins and I talked about dating, Jewish questions, my upcoming pilot with Hello Sunshine, and how the heck we'd get back to New York City. Finally, the family driver loaded me, my Torah, and several other guests back into the Escalade and we made our slow snowy journey back to the city.

As if on cue, within a few days I got a text message from Leslye, Harrison's mother. She wanted to talk with me about Harrison and Miranda's wedding ceremony and holding conversion classes with Miranda. While some would see this as meddling, I can assure you, Leslye would be anyone's dream mother-in-law. She is patient, non-judgmental, and flexible. She's glamorous while being down to earth. We chatted on the phone for a while; she told me how much she loved her daughter-in-law-to-be and how in love Harrison has always been with Miranda. Leslye was from a typical Jewish upbringing in the 1970s. She belonged to a Reform temple and brought her sons through the bar mitzvah process. I detected that she was a bit surprised that two out of her three boys found love outside of the Jewish faith. She was reassured that Harrison and Miranda had agreed to raise their children Jewish. What gave her even more comfort was that Miranda voiced interest in becoming a Jew. Leslye didn't want to pressure Miranda but desired the conversion complete before the wedding.

I got off the phone, unsure if I was ready for the task at hand. I was comfortable teaching Miranda for conversion and thought she was an excellent candidate. I knew that their wedding was in eight months and typically that is too short of a time to meaningfully convert. Typically, an Orthodox conversion of a woman takes about two years. A woman is expected to start following the laws of Judaism, join a Jewish community, learn prayers, Jewish history, and Hebrew. The conversion ceremony is sealed in front of a tribunal of rabbis, asking a few questions, making sure this person has prepared, and accepts their role as a Jew. The convert will dunk three times in the ritual bath known as a mikvah. After that, they are Jewish, given a Hebrew name, and they are expected to uphold the customs and *mitzvot*. A Reform conversion is much more loose—and often involves going to a class once a week for a year, learning units of study on lifecycle moments, holidays, and Jewish history. With Reform conversion, there is no requirement for upholding the commandments, though doing so is strongly encouraged. Finding a conversion class in the city is difficult for a lot of busy New Yorkers in a time crunch. The personal trainer/personal rabbi route makes a lot of sense. I had done it before and I was happy to do it again. I could relate to Miranda and lived in the same neighborhood; I was going to be a great teacher for her. But I didn't like the nagging feeling that if I couldn't realistically fit in all the lessons and learning needed for authentic conversion by their November wedding, then I'd be helping to facilitate an interfaith marriage. I wasn't even sure if the family had a long-time West Chester rabbi they were using for the wedding, and I was just there for the conversion. *One step at a time*, I thought to myself. I had been asked constantly to perform interfaith marriages and it was something I was *not* willing to do. Refusing to officiate intermarriage was one of *my* rabbinic boundaries. I have several cousins and friends who were intermarried and I've welcomed those new partners with openness, however I drew a line in my professional capacity.

I started working with Miranda almost every week for hour-long sessions that would turn into two-hour hangouts with my dog and lively discussions. There was no better student than Miranda. I had a syllabus that followed both Jewish holidays as they came up in the calendar, the history of Judaism, basic prayers, and lifecycle moments with practical customs that go along with the events. Harrison would sit in for about eighty-five percent of the lessons. He and Miranda enjoyed doing almost everything together, and there was a special sparkle in Harrison's eye when he saw Miranda grasp onto a concept and accept it into her heart. Sometimes, Miranda would start a session with several questions linked to assigned reading and make connections to things she had seen at Harrison's house over the years or at her church Sunday school. She was touched by symbolism, meaningful stories, the oppression of our people, and tangible customs that had purpose behind them. The couple also wanted to talk about their wedding—the *why* behind the Jewish customs of contracts, circling seven times, and the veil. Miranda wanted to know about the ins and out of conversion and its history. We went through the timeline of history from 5,800 years ago until the present. Honestly, it was exhausting because there was so much to cover and Miranda and Harrison were curious people. We'd never finish a conversation, and instead I'd leave saying "to be contin*jew*ed."

A question that arose during our classes was "Why should Miranda be a Jew if strict observance and practice isn't that important to Harrison?" Harrison and his family celebrated like a typical Reform family but they were probably more devout in their New York Giants allegiance than to Jewish religious observance. However, identity and tradition were deeply ingrained in all of the members of their family—their expression was tied mostly to culture or lifecycle moments. Some of the family's happiest times were during their Jewish upbringing and celebrations. Likewise, Harrison was very engaged when we would talk about Israel, the Holocaust, or antisemitism; while it was something Miranda could not understand firsthand, Harrison voiced connection to the Jewish people's ability to survive and rebuild in the face of hate and destruction. The palpable rise in antisemitism since the Pittsburgh synagogue shooting was something Harrison wanted to make sure that Miranda felt equally affected by too. This was impossible, and Miranda always felt like she was an imposter or coming up short, but she did her best.

I checked in with Leslye after the sessions and encouraged her that her "kids" were so engaged. I really believed Miranda would convert before the wedding. I suggested we start looking at a date that would accommodate all of the other pressing timeline items they had in their wedding plans.

During one of our discussions about their wedding details, I said "your rabbi will do xyz at your service." Harrison stopped me and said, "Aren't *you* the rabbi?" Leslye had never come out and asked me officially and we hadn't set a date for the conversion. I felt a little frozen and backed into a corner. Of course I was their rabbi, but I wasn't comfortable with intermarriage. I looked at Miranda's beautiful, soulful eyes. I had the same feeling in that moment as when I see a newborn—that it is a total lottery of life that I was born into my family and she was born into hers. She was longing for Jewish belonging, and she was doing everything to show her dedication. As their friend and rabbi, how could I desert this couple midway through the journey? I thought of how crushing that would be for Miranda as if me saying no would carry a message of: "You did an *okay* job at studying, but you'll never be Jewish *enough* for me or this family." I wanted her to feel positive every step of the way so that she would continue towards conversion and towards building a happy Jewish home. I also believed that they were in love and belonged together. Harrison was a supportive partner and Miranda was the same if not more. In the flash of all of these thoughts, my eyes teared up. I happily accepted the role of becoming their officiating rabbi for their November wedding.

We would continue learning but the sessions shifted to mostly include wedding details. We focused on the order and the ins and outs of their chuppah ceremony. One night, Miranda and Harrison came over to my rooftop with a bottle of kosher wine. We lived around the corner from each other so it was easy to spend time together. I remember I was freezing and Miranda was so warm she was sweating. I cannot recall the substance of what she was saying. What I remember is that she felt pressure like she missed the deadline and Miranda hated disappointing people. I saw so much of myself in her. Her desire to be perfect, constantly performing, pushing aside her own needs, showing up for everyone, and sometimes ending the day feeling depleted. Whatever I said on the roof had to help take the edge off. The couple needed to take some of the air out of their balloon before it popped, and it meant that conversion would be tabled until after the wedding. I never addressed this fully with Leslye for a few reasons. I didn't want to give space for disappointment in my work or disappointment in Harrison and Miranda. It seemed clear that this family was not extreme; there was no ultimatum on the table. It would be a little bummer that we couldn't get it done before the wedding, but in due time, we could bring Miranda into the religion.

I would work with Miranda's stepfather, Don, a former officer of the US Air Force, to co-officiate the wedding. Don lived in Wisconsin, so our meetings were conducted over Zoom. He brought a bright, masculine, and secular flair to the process. He was equally as curious and respectful of the Jewish customs as his stepdaughter. He'd mention over and over that he had gone to India for a wedding; being part of a Jewish wedding seemed equally exotic—though I can assure you it is *not*. Don's knowledge of Miranda and Harrison was of course more personal than mine. His fatherly advice added a special touch to the service. We worked together to script and craft the wedding ceremony.

Harrison and Miranda got married under the beautiful crisp November sky of Harrison's parent's country club. The ceremony was entirely traditional and Jewish. Other than having a female rabbi, a non-Jewish bride, and non-kosher food, everything was kosher. To be honest, this is the way more than seventy percent of American non-Orthodox Jewish weddings happen. Harrison and Miranda had a traditional ketubah that we signed with male witnesses. In order to have a ketubah, Miranda needed to choose a Hebrew name. After our discussions, I asked Miranda to consult with her parents, as parents normally bestow a name upon their children to affect their destiny. Together they chose the Hebrew name of *Rivka*. Rebecca, in English, Rivka is the lovely and kind matriarch who over-extends herself to strangers and agrees to leave her homeland and marry Isaac in Canaan. Rebecca was also Miranda's mother's name, so it was a way of naming herself after her mother—a much more *goyish,* non-Jewish, practice. RIVKA was also the name of Miranda's favorite shoe style within the fashion brand for which she worked. It all seemed like a perfect fit.

Right before the chuppah ceremony, we held an intimate gathering of just the bridal party for the ketubah signing. I sang a welcome song, explained the formality of the customs ahead, and all documents were signed. Miranda and Harrison's parents had a chance to bless their children. Harrison placed Miranda's veil over her face in an act called a *bedeken*, making sure that she was his proper bride. This was actually my favorite part of their service because it was small and sweet. There was so much love and emotion in the air when we sang a closing prayer to cap this part of the wedding. Then, a male event planner started calling out all of our names and telling us where to stand. It was like we were a chorus line of dancing show people about to perform. The weather had held up and we were going to do our service on the lawn overlooking the golf course. We lined up for the aisle processional and waited in a holding barn right behind the seated audience of two hundred guests. Miranda started to breath heavily and went to sit down in her glamorous white ball gown. We were waiting for a while, and I walked over to check on her. It was then I realized she was in distress. She seemed to have lost a sense of calm and focus that we had achieved together in the ketubah signing. She was nervous and anxious. Then, in an act of defiance, she said that she didn't want to wear her veil over her face. I don't recall if she said it or not, but I knew it made her feel trapped. Religiously, we had planned for her to wear the veil for most of the ceremony; Harrison was to lift the veil after the first cup of wine. While this was a change in plan and a departure from the traditional custom we had agreed to observe, I loved watching Miranda speak up for herself. So much of this wedding was on Harrison's home turf at their family country club, and designed according to his family's desires. Miranda had a moment to take control over how she felt and I loved it. I told her she didn't have to do anything she didn't want and feel was authentic. Woman to woman, a female rabbi to bride, she nodded and I watched her shake off the panic of a little girl. She was stepping into the role of a woman by making a definitive choice. My ability to be flexible and supportive gave her the boost to do it.

I prayed for Harrison and Miranda as she circled seven times in her RIVKA shoes. The circles represent the bride creating protection for their union as well as removing any walls or final barriers she has before they conquer each other and become one unit. I may have lost count during the circling and I think she did too. I said a quick prayer for myself as well, under their fragrant and fresh canopy that I would one day stand under the same structure and find my *bashert*, intended. (Ben and I had our first date already scheduled four days later.) I watched Miranda intently during the chuppah. Harrison was the same Guy Smiley he had always been. He was happy and shining. Miranda's usual glow was ultraradiant. Although it trembled with emotion, her voice was loud and clear as she read her vows. She looked to me occasionally for assurance during the ceremony. But she was actually in charge. The ceremony was picture perfect and everyone was incredibly happy. Below are Miranda's vows she swore to Harrison:

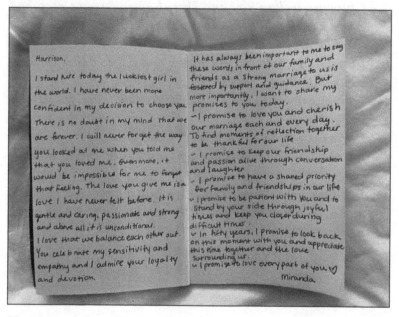

Harrison,

I stand here today the luckiest girl in the world. I have never been more confident in my decision to choose you. There is no doubt in my mind that we are forever. I will never forget the way you looked at me when you told me that you love me. Even more, it would be impossible for me to forget that feeling. The love you give me is a love I have never felt before. It is gentle and caring, passionate and strong, and above all it is unconditional. I love that we balance each other out. You celebrate my sensitivity and empathy and I admire your loyalty and devotion. It has always been important to me to say these words in front of our family and friends as a strong marriage to us is fostered by support and guidance. But more importantly, I want to share my promises to you today.

~*I promise to love you and cherish our marriage each and every day. To find moments of reflection together to be thankful for our Life.*

~*I promise to keep our friendship and passion alive through conversation and laughter.*

~*I promise to have a shared priority for family and friendships in our life.*

~*I promise to be patient with you and to stand by your side through joyful times and keep you closer during difficult times.*

~*In fifty years, I promise to look back on this moment with you and appreciate this time together and the love surrounding us.*

~*I promise to love every part of you* ❤

Miranda

This couple have become my lifelong friends. I officiated over the marriage of their first cousins and also Harrison's brother, Justin, within six months of their wedding. Together, we have danced many times, including at my own wedding. They still live around the block from me and recently adopted a golden retriever named Oakely. Scout and Oakley even have gone on walks together. Miranda was the first non-Jew to reach out during October 7th and the ensuing war to ask how I was doing and express solidarity with the Jewish people. Miranda is still interested in converting though she stopped classes with me after her wedding.

I think Miranda is a remarkable person for choosing to braid her life and soul to the fabric of our people. She bakes challah, celebrates holidays, and sacrifices her desires for the greater good of her family unit. That she does so without giving guilt-trips is perhaps the most non-Jewish part about her. It is not an easy choice to love someone different from your upbringing, and we cannot ignore the uphill journey of interfaith partners. They start out not fully accepted. That an expectation was put upon Miranda to master Judaism by a certain deadline in order to marry to the love of her life was perhaps antiquated and unfair. However, to be fair, it was on the table from day one, that Miranda was falling in love with a Jew and their blending would be an issue. It is not my desire to seek out work to officiate over interfaith marriage ceremonies. Still, I know that I will continue to meet couples that are exceptions to my rules and will allow my practice to evolve for couples that demonstrate a commitment to building a Jewish home together. I will always support existing interfaith families and Jewish allies. That may seem contradictory and convoluted, and in some ways it is. It is also part of my privilege as an independent private provider to update and change my practices the way I see as authentic to my beliefs. With open arms, I will help people with meaningful conversion—even if just within the more flexible and Reform movement, and then facilitate a marriage. (I warn potential converts that converting in any process outside of the Orthodox movement will impact whether they are universally accepted as a Jew). I encourage and support Jews marrying Jews for the best hope of bringing up deeply Jewish identifying children and continuing our people. However, I believe there are many ways to raise proud Jewish children from interfaith marriages.

There is no doubt as to how much Harrison and Miranda are committed to their relationship. I believe that love is love and it can exist between people from different backgrounds. I am married to an Australian, who is different from me in multiple facets. Yet, it will always be somewhat of a challenge for Harrison and Miranda to navigate when there are current events that hit one of them harder than the other. Raising their children Jewishly will be a task Miranda will try so hard to nail, and along the way, I'm sure she will come up against undermining comments for not being born a Jew. With respect to this, I have advised Miranda that I'm not positive she'll feel differently *even after* she has converted. I don't even think the comments will come from her supportive in-laws, but from the community at large and deep within herself. Feeling like you don't belong is a terrible feeling. No mother or partner wants to feel inadequate. We all have confidence issues and there will always be a dynamic setting the convert up to prove themselves. I feel for Miranda as she continues on her journey to learn more about Judaism and see if she truly wants to convert.

As a rabbi, it is important to stay supportive, open and flexible for the families we serve. It is impossible to be a modern rabbi in America and not come across interfaith couples. They are not going anywhere and if we want Judaism to survive, it must adapt and so too must institutions. To be masterful representatives of the religion, rabbis and officiants need to extend loving kindness in order to navigate the obstacles in front of every future marriage. We have to be part of the solution and help use the traditions as our guides.

CONFESSION XI:
Even though I respect Jewish law,
I hate being told what to do.

"She sets her mind on a field and acquires it . . . she plants a
vineyard through the fruit of her handiwork."
—*ESHET CHAYIL*. KING SOLOMON

At my Grandma Rev's funeral, I learned that she thought that the traditional Sabbath song, "Woman of Valor," was sexist and anti-feminist. It prescribes all the things that a "good woman" should do for her family. Of course, my grandmother was an excellent daughter, sister, wife, mother, and grandmother. She was the typical Jewish matriarch. But because she didn't appreciate the way the text insists a worthy woman serves her husband, the Eisenstadt family never sang *Eshet Chayil* as part of their family practice. I didn't learn the verses until I was a twenty year old and spent time in more religious social circles. When I learned that my grandmother never really loved the prayer, it reminded me of a satirical article my grandmother sent me when I was in college about women's liberation. She was not a feminist, but also not a 1950s housewife. Grandma Rev was actually a Girl Scout and troop leader. She believed in their mission to build up communities of courageous and confident women. My first cousin, Jessica Rosenberg Levy, is a passionate continuation of the Girl Scout tradition in our family— having attended all of the camps and programs even abroad to help women and girls. Grandma Rev was a moderate and wasn't extreme one way or another. My grandma taught me to believe in my own efforts, strong values, and mind my business. She kept confidences and did not meddle in other people's affairs. Grandma Rev led with warmth and love, nurturing and hard work, but also had boundaries that were passed down to her ten grandchildren, including myself.

Once a person stops limiting themselves with expectations of others and societal norms (cultural or religious), the possibilities are endless. So many people think that religion is about restrictions. Like the Girl Scouts, Judaism is a blueprint of values to build character. Judaism provides a calendar and behavioral framework by which to live. By now, you have read that I am honest; I keep it real and follow only what sits authentically with me. I used to think there was no way a woman could do all the things that I do in the religious world. I don't push others to think like me and respect the people who don't want a female provider. Still, I know that I can and will continue to help people "get Jewish." I've been a help in keeping our religion alive. I teach our religion and offer the opinions of the strictest forms and continually remind my students there are many ways to accept the laws and customs of Judaism. After all, I am a *female* rabbi, so I have chosen to accept some of the rules and de facto ignored others.

What's next for me? I want to enjoy my first years of marriage and build a family. I want to honeymoon in Italy just like my sister did with her husband and my brother did with his wife. Ben and I long to return to the south of Israel and continue the work of building relationships between peaceful Israelis and Palestinians. We hope to start more ethical businesses that are good for the environment, our people, and all peoples. A shameless brag about Ben—in the late spring of 2024, The Good Charcoal Company, for which Ben serves as CEO and cofounder, was named one of the TIME100 Most Influential Businesses. The Good Charcoal Company makes barbecue charcoal from invasive acacia bush in

Africa, and in doing so, restores cheetah habitat and grass lands for carbon capture. His company hosts bi-monthly cookouts for food insecure Americans and by June 2024 has served 50,000 free meals nationwide. The all-natural charcoal and its farming process led to The Good Charcoal Company winning the Forest Stewardship Council's 2023 Leadership Award. His premium lump was named best overall charcoal for grilling by *Food and Wine Magazine* two years in a row. I am so proud of him and his hard work with cofounder Rob Silverman and dedicated staff. My husband and I want to be a team that compliments each other and ultimately draws each other closer to G-d and our true purposes.

I long to name children after my grandparents and mentor Liz, and raise them in ways that they would have been proud of. I want to show my children first hand where they come from and the values that were passed to me from my parents and grandparents. I want to teach them to love with words and action. I want them to know the importance of giving in order to receive inner-fulfillment. I want them to be confident and silly, multifaceted, and whatever they want. Most of all, I really just long to fulfill that first command in the Bible, to procreate.

I want to be a woman of valor on my terms. I want to work hard and see the fruits of my labor. Whether that's in my career with my families or in writing, I know I will stay on track and continue my important work. As a religious leader that is outside of the mainstream institutional organizations, I hope I will have a seat at the large round table when leaders come together to brainstorm for change and best practices for a Jewish future. I hope to be a big drop in the bucket that will fight antisemitism with positive Jewish figures doing good in the world. I hope to add to the complexity of Jewish identity in America, and show much more of the flexibility and the fun.

What's more, I hope to be a successful disruptor and deliver religion to more people in dynamic ways. Brands like Uber and Netflix have figured out how to bring customers exactly *what* they want, *when* they want it. Religion is suffering and needs a disruptive boost too. The outdated model will become obsolete in a few generations, and I cannot sit idly by and watch that happen to G-d's beautiful teachings. I am a changemaker, providing access to spirituality and religious practice. I hope to inspire others to evolve like me.

EPILOGUE

Here are my Ten Commandments—or Ten suggested behaviors that can help readers stay close to G-d and religion without feeling suffocated. They include ways to introduce and maintain simple rituals, share blessings that bring gratitude, and cultivate a sense of identity. Hopefully they leave you with joy and a desire for more.

1. Always make an advance plan for observance. Don't leave it to spontaneity. If you fail to plan, you plan to fail.

2. Start small. Choose one ritual that you can perform weekly or monthly. For both women and men, I would suggest lighting Sabbath candles and saying an intentional blessing over all the things you created and your hopes for the restful weekend ahead.

3. Wear something outwardly Jewish. Is it a chain you got from your grandmother? A Jewish Star necklace? A gift from a bar or bat mitzvah? A *chai pendant,* symbolizing life? Keep your Jewish identity on you at all times, as a physical reminder. There are great Jewish jewelry designers out there if you don't have anything yet: I recommend Rachie Shnay's pieces.

4. Lean into the next holiday. If you are reading this during the new year, really go for what it means to start fresh and let go of bad behaviors. If you are reading during Hanukkah time, light candles all eight nights and eat the holiday foods. The more you practice one holiday the more it will lead to more.

5. Read. Read. Read. You never stop learning about Jewish subjects. Read about Israel and the Arab-Israeli conflict. Read about Jewish culture. Read opinion pieces. One article and one source is never enough. I have subscriptions to Audible, *Haaretz*, Audiobooks. com, *Washington Post*, *New York Times*, *Bloomberg*, and *Wall Street Journal*. Opinions I enjoy hearing come from Rabbi Joseph Telushkin, Michael J. Oren, Thomas Friedman, Rich Cohen, Noa Tishby, Rabbi Elliot Cosgrove, Rabbi Sharon Brous, and many others. Do not limit yourself to obtaining information only through soundbite sources like YouTube, TikTok, and Instagram.

6. Linked to number five, know your history. If you don't know where you come from, how could you possibly know where you are going? If your parents or schooling failed you, teach yourself or find a class.

7. Get involved in charity. To help the widow, the stranger, or the orphan is a common command in the Jewish Bible. There is a need. You have something to give. Every organization needs money and you must give of yourself. The more you practice giving the more you will give. This was a guiding principle of

the Lubavitcher Rebbe and I fully pass it on to all who listen.

8. Respect your parents. Instill that respect in your own children or the children around you.

9. In your friendships and partnerships, make room for your religion. Make sure you have friends that have similar values and openly discuss your values with friends. This will help you create your own *kehilah* or community if institutions aren't appealing. Plan holidays, charity gatherings, study groups, and the like. They can be either Jewish or interfaith groups.

10. Find a way to be happy with your own portion. Look deep into your own heart and account for the blessings that you have, the life you were given, and the potential of the future that is yours for the taking.

This is the foundation. These are the musts and/or the takeaways from meaningful Jewish life. They are both what you need to start and the lasting effects of starting. The last Jewish value I will pass on, for now, is *zerizut*, fulfilling obligations at the proper time and with urgency. There is no time like the present. Start, don't hesitate. You'll end up hungry for more. You'll start to follow some Jewish influencers, read more, maybe even seek out a community, synagogue, or private educator.

"Get relig," as I would say. Just do *something*, and more will come later.

Peace in the Middle East. To be contin*JE*Wed.

ACKNOWLEDGMENTS

This memoir has been a work in the making for my whole life. I must acknowledge the many people who contributed to my thoughts and writing through supportive relationships.

(As an aside, this part of the book feels like the end of my own bat mitzvah speech.)

My fantastic family starts with my parents, Merry and David Eisenstadt, and grandparents, all of blessed memory, Revelyn and Jack Eisenstadt and Bette and Ralph K. Madway. A special thanks to my mother for giving me feedback, writer-to-writer, and I apologize for not taking the suggestions she shared and going for the cover she didn't prefer. Thank you to my siblings and in-laws Rachel Eisenstadt German and Steven German, Eli Eisenstadt and Celia Feuer, Henry and Sonia Jablonski, and Natalie Rushiniak and Lisa Jablonski. I am thankful to my siblings' supportive in-laws, Ronnie and Arthur German and Gerald and Judy Feuer. I am so grateful to my aunts and uncles: Susan and Jeffery Dreifuss; Gail and Frank McHugh; Sue and Stan Levin; and Bill and Linda Madway; honorary aunts and uncles: Shelley and Peter Dreifuss; Anath and Moshe Flugelman; Ruth and Ami Tal; and Issac Zaksenberg; and my troves of cousins who helped to make my Jewish upbringing even sweeter and broadened my acceptance for interfaith marriages. A special thank you to Joshua and Toula Dreifuss for allowing me to share their story in my opening chapter.

To all the families who have ever entrusted me with their

family's Jewish education or lifecycle moments: thank you. You took a chance on a young rabbi with strong opinions and a dog that never left her side. You helped me build my community as I honed my practice and contributed to the many stories in this book. Thank you specifically to the Dayan-Lindemanns, Goulds, Kaskels, Krolls, Rabins, Rices, Romo-Edelmans, Sotoloffs, and Weiners. All those listed, in addition to many others are like family and role models. Beyond always encouraging me to become a Rabbi: Your love supported me, your constant giving inspired me, and your children filled my heart and sense of belonging. As I have worked with hundreds of families and students, it is impossible to list everyone. Still, I must make a special mention to the Mitchells, Fodemans, Kalikows, Liptons, and Veronas.

Thank you to my many professional collaborators: Rabbi Rachel Rosenbluth (Bluth), Jerome Korman, Rabbi Mira Rivera, Arielle Korman, Joel Cohen, Daniella Rabbani, Andrew Greenberger, Naamah Imir, David Hertzberg, Paul Shapiro, Meg Okura, Noah Solomon Chase, and Yoshi Fruchter. Thank you to all the synagogues that partner with me and allow me to teach their members and student. A special thank you to Door to Toor Tutoring and Congregation Habonim. Thank you to Melissa and Janet of Gourmet Advisory Serives, Dayna Field, Keren Precel Events, Total Entertainment, Lawrence Scott Events, Emlan Events, and others. Thank you to Hello Sunshine, Sue Kinkead, and Alisa Singer for the brief and exciting time that I thought I'd have a TV show. Thank you for the opportunities and mentorship from Matthew Motl Didner and Zalmen Mlotek of the National Yiddish Theatre Folksbiene, and Kolya Borodulin for teaching me Yiddish. Thank you for the many lessons learned while working with Broadway producer Richard Frankel and 54 Below. Though we've yet to meet, thank you to Andy Cohen and Adam Sandler for being unabashedly

Jewish and modern and for providing me with endless nights of entertainment.

I am grateful for inspirational leaders in the New York Jewish community (whether they realize I learned from them or not) like Rabbi Angela Buchdahl, Cantor Julia Cadrain, Rabbi Naftali Citron, Rabbi Elliot J. Cosgrove PhD, Rabbi David Gelfand, Cantor Bruce Halev, Rabbi David Ingber, Rabbi Dianne Kohler-Esses, Rabbi Yehuda Lipsker, Rabbi Adam Mintz, Rabbi Avram Mlotek, Rabbi Laurie Phillips (z"l), Rabbi Dan Ross, Hazzan Basya Schechter, Rabbi Mark Wildes, Rabbi Yoseph Wilhelm, Rabbi Neil Zuckerman, among others. Though I've never met them, my writing and learning was influenced by great modern rabbis like Rabbi Sharon Brous, Rabbi Joseph Telushkin, and Rabbi David Wolpe. I have deep gratitude to the leaders I grew up with: Cantor Abraham Lubin, Rabbi Lyle Fishman, Rabbi Jonathan Maltzman, and Rabbi William Rudolph (z"l). Thank you to my many teachers from the Charles E. Smith Jewish Day School, especially Rabbi Reuven Greenvald and Yoram Bar-Noy. Thank you to Rabbi Charles Agin at Mesifta Adas Wolkowisk. Thank you to NYU Tisch School of the Arts, including Liz Swados, of blessed memory.

My neighbors, Sabrina Benun and Remy Zeitoune, have provided and continue to provide me and so many others with strong and consistent Jewish community. Thank you for involving me in The Food Connection, preparing and delivering thousands of kosher meals in partnership with multiple Jewish organizations and Sephardic Bikkur Cholim. Thank you to Robbie Brenner, Executive Director of AFINS, for your years of leadership and support. Thank you to Kibbutz Samar and the entire family of Building Together. Thank you to the UJA, Taglit-Birthright and Jewish National Fund, especially for organizing my volunteer mission in Israel post October 7th. Supporting these charitable institutions helped me to fulfill *mitzvot*, commandments, and my purpose.

Thank you to Start Publishing's Viva Editions, to Jarred Weisfeld and Ashley Calvano for their tireless work on this book, its editing, and ensuring its quality. Thank you to Alex Korolkovas for shooting the cover photo that artfully captures my spirit, glamor, and humor. Thank you to Rina Gluckman for the beautiful photo on the back cover. Thank you to Jennifer Do for the great graphic design. Thank you to Scott Kaufman, my agent at Don Buchwald and Associates, for your friendship and championing this project and others. Thank you to Dan Sirkin for expert your legal and contract work. To Sheryl and Carrie Berk, thank you for helping me along the way and being a role models in the writing world.

To my friends, Liz, Noa, Oran, Svetlana, Daniella, Aaron, Arienne, Tom, Kathy, Larry, Latreal, Leon, Farin, Harper, Julie, Spencer, Parker, Phoebe, Jenny, Cindy, Lynn, Renée, Rivke, Shira, and Alon: thanks for listening to me go on and on about the book, Israel, and the wedding.

To my dog, Scout: you make countless children happy to learn about their religion and provide me with unconditional love. You are the sweetest creature.

To my husband, Ben: Thank you. You're my world and my true partner.

Modah ani, I am thankful to G-d for the opportunity to write this book, exercise Judaism in the way I choose and inspire others. Oh, and thank you to Barbra Streisand. Just because.

Lastly, thank *you* for reading this book and exploring an interest in the evolution of religion. Thank you for allowing me to share these transformational stories through faith and ritual. Thank you for helping me tell my story. I hope you enjoyed reading *Confessions of a Female Rabbi.*